# WOMEN OF THE BIBLE: STRENGTH, FAITH AND LEGACY

*BY PASTOR JOSÉ ARNALDO LIMA SOCARRÁS*

*Women of the Bible: Strength, Faith and Legacy / José Arnaldo Lima Socarrás.*

*"May every page of this book inspire and strengthen you, reflecting the faith and courage of the women of the Bible, and may their stories transform your life as they have mine."*

*Luz María Barrera Castillo.*

*"On the journey of faith, may you find in the lives of these women a beacon of hope and a witness to God's faithfulness, guiding your journey with courage and purpose."*

*Luz María Barrera Castillo.*

# DEDICATION

To my wife Lucy, for her love and affection, her desire to see that everything goes according to God's desire, she finds in these women an example of dedication and fidelity.

*JOSÉ ARNALDO LIMA SOCARRÁS.*

# CONTENT

| | |
|---|---|
| PROLOGUE | 7 |
| INTRODUCTION | 9 |
| CHAPTER I PATRIARCHAL PERIOD | 12 |
|    EVA –THE MOTHER OF ALL– | 12 |
|    SARA –THE MOTHER OF NATIONS– | 15 |
|    REBECA – A WOMAN OF DECISION | ¡Error! Marcador no definido. |
|    RAQUEL AND LEA – BROTHERHOOD AND RIVALRY | 23 |
| CHAPTER II TERM OF JUDGES | 27 |
|    MIRIAM – LEADERSHIP AND WORSHIP | 27 |
|    DEBORAH –THE PROPHETESS AND JUDGE– | 31 |
|    JAEL – THE BRAVE WOMAN – | 35 |
|    RUTH – LOYALTY AND REDEMPTION | 39 |
|    NAOMI – THE FAITHFUL MOTHER-IN-LAW | 43 |
| CHAPTER III MONARCHICAL PERIOD | 47 |
|    HANNAH – PRAYER AND PROMISE | 47 |
|    ABIGAIL –WISE AND PEACEFUL WOMAN– | 51 |
|    BATHSHEBA – FROM SINNER TO QUEEN MOTHER | 55 |
|    THE QUEEN OF SHEBA – WISDOM AND WEALTH | 59 |
|    RISPA –MOURNING AND JUSTICE– | ¡Error! Marcador no definido. |
|    HULDAH THE PROPHETESS OF KING JOSIAH | 67 |
| CHAPTER IV PERIOD OF EXILE AND RETURN | 71 |
|    ESTHER –COURAGE AND PROVIDENCE– | 71 |
|    THE WIDOW OF SAREPTA – FAITH AND PROVISION | ¡Error! Marcador no definido. |
|    THE SHUNAMMITE WOMAN – FAITH AND RESURRECTION | 79 |
|    SUSANA –JUSTICE AND PURITY– | 83 |
| CHAPTER V INTERTESTAMENTAL PERIOD | 87 |
|    JUDITH –COURAGE AND STRATEGY– | 87 |

*WOMAN OF THE MACCABEES – COURAGE AND FAITH –* .................. 91
CHAPTER VI PERIOD OF THE NEW TESTAMENT .................................................. **95**
*MARY – THE MOTHER OF JESUS –* ....................................................... 95
*ELISABETH – THE MOTHER OF JOHN THE BAPTIST –* ....................... 99
*ANNA, PROPHETESS – HOPE AND DEVOTION* ................................. 103
*MARTA –SERVE WITH HOSPITALITY–* ............................................... 107
*MARY OF BETHANY – DEVOTION IN ADORATION* ......................... 111
*MARY MAGDALENE – WITNESS OF THE RESURRECTION* ................. 116
*THE WOMAN WITH THE ISSUE OF BLOOD – FAITH AND HEALING* 120
*THE SYROPHOENICIAN WOMAN – FAITH AND PERSEVERANCE* ..... 124
*THE SAMARITAN WOMAN – FAITH AND TRANSFORMATION* ........ 128
*PRISCILA – COLLABORATOR IN THE MINISTRY –* ........................... 132
*PHOEBE –THE HELPFUL DEACONESS–* ............................................. 136
*LIDIA –FIRST CONVERTED IN EUROPE–*. **¡Error! Marcador no definido.**
*DORCAS (TABITH) – LIFE OF SERVICE AND RESURRECTION* ............. 144
*JUANA – FOLLOWER AND BENEFACTOR OF JESUS* ......................... 148
*RHODA –THE MAID WHO LISTENED TO PEDRO–* ........................... 152
*THE WOMAN WITH THE SPIRIT OF SICKNESS – HEALING AND LIBERATION* ....................................................................................... 156
*THE ADULTEROUS WOMAN – FORGIVENESS AND RETAURATION* –160
*SUSANA –SUPPORT AND SERVICE IN THE MINISTRY–* .................... 164
*EUNICE AND LOIS – TRANSGENERATIONAL FAITH–* .. **¡Error! Marcador no definido.**
*JUNIAS – APOSTLE OF CHRIST–* ........................................................ 171
FINAL CONCLUSIONS AND REFLECTIONS ................................................ 175
*FINAL PRAYER:* ......................................................................................... 176
APPENDICES .................................................................................................. 177
  **Appendix 1: Relevant Historical Documents** ............................... 177
  **Appendix 2: Key Bible Verse Lists** ................................................. 177
  **Appendix 3: Diagrams and Tables** ................................................ 178

*Women of the Bible: Strength, Faith and Legacy / José Arnaldo Lima Socarrás.*

*NOTES* .................................................................................... **180**
   **Important observation** ............................................... 183
*GLOSSARY* ............................................................................ **184**
*BIBLIOGRAPHY* ................................................................... **186**
*AUTHOR BIOGRAPHY* ........................................................ **188**
    **Education and Career** .................................................... 188
    **Works and Contributions** ............................................... 188
    **International Ministry** ................................................... 189
    **Personal Life** ................................................................. 189
*WORKS OF THE AUTHOR* .................................................. **190**
*FINAL ENDPAPERS* ............................................................ **193**

# PROLOGUE

### A Journey of Faith and Fortitude

Throughout biblical history, women have played pivotal roles that have left a lasting legacy, inspiring generations of believers. From Eve's bravery to Mary's devotion, each of these women faced unique challenges with unwavering faith, making their mark on the narrative of redemption. My dear husband, José Arnaldo Lima Socarrás, offers us in "Women of the Bible: Strength, Faith and Legacy" a profound reflection on these extraordinary lives.

### The Relevance of Biblical Women

Women's stories in the Bible are much more than ancient stories; they are living testimonies of God's power in the midst of adversity and the transforming impact of faith. Each chapter of this book examines the life of a biblical woman, providing historical context, analyzing her challenges and triumphs, and drawing spiritual lessons that remain pertinent to our lives today.

### A Legacy of Faith and Strength

From Eve, the mother of all, whose error reminds us of the need for divine grace, to Mary, the mother of Jesus, whose yes to God changed the course of history, these women teach us about human nature and God's faithfulness. This book celebrates his legacy and invites us to reflect on our own life and faith.

### Reflections and Practical Applications

Knowing the stories is just the beginning; It is vital to allow its lessons to transform our lives. At the end of each chapter, you'll find insights and practical applications designed to help you apply biblical teachings in your daily life. Also included are model prayers and reflection questions to encourage personal time of meditation and spiritual growth.

### Invitation to Readers

I invite you to join this journey of discovery and growth. Allow the stories of these women of the Bible to inspire, challenge, and strengthen you in your own walk of faith. My hope is that, as you read about their lives, you will find a deeper connection with God and a greater understanding of your own calling and purpose in His redemptive plan.

With love and blessings,

Luz María Barrera Castillo.

# INTRODUCTION

"Women of the Bible: Strength, Faith and Legacy".

Women have played an essential role in biblical history, and their stories offer rich teachings about faith, strength, and legacy. From the first pages of the Bible, we see how God uses courageous and faithful women to carry out His divine purposes. This book seeks to explore these stories, not only to remember their contributions, but to learn from their experiences and apply those lessons in our own lives.

The book, "Women of the Bible: Strength, Faith, and Legacy," aims to delve into the lives of these remarkable women, examine the challenges they faced, and highlight their faith and courage. In doing so, we intend to provide a resource that inspires and builds up, showing how God's faithfulness is manifested through the lives of those who trust in Him.

This book covers a variety of key female figures in the Bible, from the Old Testament to the New Testament. Each chapter focuses on a specific woman, providing historical context, examining their challenges and triumphs, and reflecting on the spiritual lessons we can learn from their lives. Through this exploration, we hope that readers will find inspiration and strength to face their own challenges with faith and trust in God.

The key themes that we will address in this book are recurrent in the stories of these biblical women, in that sense, the following stand out:

- ❖ Faith and Trust in God: The importance of trusting God in the midst of difficult circumstances.
- ❖ Obedience and Submission: The courage to follow God's will even when it is difficult.
- ❖ Lasting Impact: How these women's decisions and actions have left a legacy that continues to inspire generations.
- ❖ Practical Application: How the lessons learned from these stories can be applied to our daily lives to strengthen our faith and our relationship with God.

This book, *The Women of the Bible: Strength, Faith, and Legacy*, takes a fascinating journey through the centuries, exploring the lives of extraordinary women who marked history. Through detailed study, you will discover their unique stories, the challenges and sacrifices they faced, how their faith transformed them, and how their legacy is still relevant to our lives today. It is a complete guide to immerse yourself in the lives of the women of the Bible. Divided into six chapters that correspond to the most significant periods of biblical history – Patriarchal, Judges, Monarchical, Exile and Return, Intertestamental and New Testament – this work invites us to get to know up close those women who, with their unwavering faith and courage, left an indelible mark on the people of God.

I invite you to explore the legacy of strength and faith of the women of the Bible, may these stories inspire you to live with faith and courage. Allow the stories of these women to transform your life and help you grow in your relationship with God, finding inspiration, transformation, and a call to live a life of purpose.

Blessings

José Arnaldo Lima Socarrás.

*Prayer:*

Lord Jesus, thank you for the transformation you have made in my life. Help me to share my testimony with others and to be an instrument of your love and grace. May my life reflect your transformative power.

*Amen.*

*Introduction.*

*Women of the Bible: Strength, Faith and Legacy / José Arnaldo Lima Socarrás.*

# CHAPTER I PATRIARCHAL PERIOD

## *EVE*
## *– THE MOTHER OF ALL –*

Scripture: Genesis 2:18-23; 3:1-6, 3:20

*History and Context*:

Eve was the first woman created by God, formed from Adam's rib to be his companion. Together they lived in the Garden of Eden, a paradise where they had everything they needed. However, Eve was tempted by the serpent and disobeyed God's command by eating from the tree of the knowledge of good and evil, resulting in the introduction of sin into the world.

*Challenges and Mistakes:*

Eve's greatest challenge was to face the temptation of the forbidden fruit. The serpent deceived her, and by disobeying God's command, both she and Adam were expelled from Eden. This act of disobedience had lasting consequences for all of humanity.

*Faith and Legacy:*

Despite her error, Eve is recognized as the mother of all living. His story underscores the importance of obedience to God and the gravity of sin. His life reminds us of the need for redemption and divine grace. Eve represents the beginning of human history and her legacy continues through all generations.

*Practical Applications and Reflections:*

- ❖ Consequences of Sin:
  Reflect on how our decisions can have lasting consequences. Consider areas in your life where you need to more faithfully obey God's teachings.
- ❖ Need for Redemption:
  Recognize the need for grace and redemption in your life. Seek reconciliation with God through confession and repentance.
- ❖ Obedience Lessons:
  Learn from Eve's experience the importance of obedience to God and the consequences of disobeying His word.

*Modern Relevance:*

Eve's story has lasting relevance in Christian theology and in the daily lives of believers. It represents the beginning of humanity and the introduction of sin, highlighting the need for a Savior. Eve reminds us of the importance of obedience and the constant need for divine grace.

*Examples of Modern Relevance:*

1. Fighting Temptation: **In modern life, temptations are present in many forms. Eve's story teaches us to be alert and to seek strength in God to resist temptation.**
2. Impact of Decisions: **The decisions we make not only affect us, but also those around us. Learning from Eve can guide us to make wiser and more godly decisions.**
3. Redemption and Grace: **The need for redemption shown in Eve's story is still relevant today. It reminds us that, despite our mistakes, God offers His grace and forgiveness through Jesus Christ.**

*Importance in Theology:*

Eve plays a crucial role in Christian theology as the first woman and mother of humanity. Their disobedience and the consequent fall of man establish the necessity of God's redemption and plan of salvation. God's promise in Genesis 3:15, known as the Protoevangelium, foretells the future defeat of the serpent by the offspring of the woman, pointing to Jesus Christ.

*Reflection and Group Activity:*

- Reflect on times of temptation in your life and how you have responded.
- Share strategies for applying God's teachings in daily life and pray for one another to strengthen your commitment to obedience to God.
- Discuss as a group how Eve's story highlights the need for redemption and how this relates to the coming of Christ

**Prayer:**

Lord, help us not only to hear your Word, but also to live it daily. Strengthen us to build our lives on your truth and to resist the temptations we face. May our decisions reflect your will and bring glory to your name.

*Amen.*

## Grade Sheet:

### Questions to Reflect on and Answer:

1. How can you apply Eve's obedience lessons in your daily life?

_____
_____

2. What areas of your life need reconciliation with God, and how can you seek His redemption?

3. What choices have you made that have had a lasting impact on your life or the lives of others?

4. How can you resist temptation in your daily life?

**Summary of the Previous and Next Chapter:**

- **Previous Chapter:** Introduction – Explanation of the purpose and scope of the book, and brief introduction to the key topics to be discussed.
- **Next Chapter:** Sarah - The Mother of Nations - Exploration of Sarah's life, her faith, and her role in God's promise.

---

*Chapter I. Patriarchal Period.*

# SARA
## – THE MOTHER OF NATIONS –

Scripture: Genesis 17:15-21; 21:1-7

*History and Context:*

Sarah, originally named Sarai, was Abraham's wife and Isaac's mother. God changed her name to Sarah, which means "princess," as part of His promise that she would be the mother of nations and kings. Despite his advanced age and the barrenness he had suffered for years, God promised him a son, Isaac, and he kept his promise, demonstrating his faithfulness.

*Challenges and Tests of Faith:*

Sara faced the trial of waiting and doubt. For many years, she and Abraham waited for the fulfillment of God's promise to give them a son. In a moment of weakness, Sarah suggested that Abraham have a son with his servant, Hagar, which brought conflict and complications. Eventually, however, Sarah conceived and gave birth to Isaac, proving that nothing is impossible for God.

*Faith and Legacy:*

Sarah's faith, although she had moments of weakness, is highlighted in the Bible. At Hebrews 11:11, it is mentioned that, by faith, Sarah received strength to conceive, despite her advanced age. His story underscores the importance of trusting God's promises, even when circumstances seem impossible. Sarah is considered a mother in the faith, and her legacy lives on through generations of believers.

*Practical Applications and Reflections:*

- ❖ Waiting on God:
  Reflect on the importance of waiting patiently on God's promises, even when it seems hopeless.
- ❖ Trust in God's Promises:
  Learn to trust God's promises and not let doubt lead you astray from His plan.
- ❖ Faith in the Impossible:
  Recognize that, with God, all things are possible, and that His timing is perfect.

*Modern Relevance:*

Sarah's story has lasting relevance for believers today. It teaches us to have faith in God's promises and to wait patiently for their fulfillment, even when it seems impossible.

*Examples of Modern Relevance:*

1. Faith in Times of Waiting: **People who are waiting for answers to their prayers can be inspired by Sarah's patience and faith, trusting that God will fulfill His promises in due time.**
2. Overcoming Doubt: **Sarah's story reminds us that even though we may doubt in times of difficulty, God is still faithful and can keep His promises.**
3. Modern Miracles: Testimonies of couples who have experienced the blessing of children after years of infertility can see in Sarah's story a reflection of God's power to work miracles today.

*Importance in Theology:*

Sarah is a central figure in Old Testament and New Testament theology. In the Old Testament, it is part of God's covenant with Abraham, which includes the promise of a great offspring. In the New Testament, it is mentioned as an example of faith in Hebrews 11. Her story also highlights the importance of spiritual motherhood and trust in God.

*Reflection and Group Activity:*

- Reflect on a time when you've had to wait on God and how that waiting has strengthened your faith.

- Share as a group experiences of promises fulfilled and how God has demonstrated His faithfulness.
- Pray together for those who are in times of waiting, asking God to strengthen their faith and give them patience.

***Prayer:***

Lord, strengthen our faith and patience as we wait on your promises. Help us to trust in your faithfulness and to recognize that your timing is perfect. May our lives reflect Sarah's faith and your power to do the impossible.

*Amen.*

## Grade Sheet:

### Questions to Reflect on and Answer:

1. How can you apply Sarah's patience and faith in your daily life?

2. What promises from God are you waiting for, and how can you trust His faithfulness more?

3. Have you had moments of doubt? How can you overcome those doubts with faith in God?

4. What testimonies of faith and miracles can you share to encourage others?

**Summary of the Previous and Next Chapter:**

- **Previous Chapter:** Eve - The Mother of All - Explore the creation of Eve, her role in the fall, and the importance of obedience to God.
- **Next Chapter:** Rebekah - A Woman of Decision - Discusses Rebekah's life, her choice as Isaac's wife, and her role in the story of Jacob and Esau.

*Chapter I. Patriarchal Period.*

# REBEKAH
# - A WOMAN OF DECISION -

Bible Text: Genesis 24; 27.

*History and Context:*

Rebekah, daughter of Bethuel and sister of Laban, was chosen as Isaac's wife by Abraham's servant, who had been sent to find a wife for his master's son. Rebekah demonstrated her hospitality and kindness by offering water to the servant and his camels. She agreed to leave her home and family to marry Isaac, trusting in God's guidance. Later, she became the mother of twins Jacob and Esau.

*Challenges and Decisions:*

Rebeca faced several challenges and made meaningful decisions. One of the most prominent was his role in obtaining Isaac's blessing for Jacob instead of Esau. This decision, though controversial, was crucial to the fulfillment of God's promises through Jacob, who became Israel, the father of the twelve tribes.

*Faith and Legacy:*

Rebekah's life is marked by her faith and her willingness to follow divine guidance, even in difficult circumstances. Her story underscores the importance of obedience and trust in God's plans, despite challenges. His legacy continues through his sons and his influence on Israel's history.

*Practical Applications and Reflections:*

- ❖ Obedience to God's Guidance:
  Reflect on the importance of following God's guidance in your life, even when it involves making difficult choices.
- ❖ Trust in God's Plans:
  Learn to trust God's plans for your life, recognizing that His perspective is broader than ours.
- ❖ Family Influence:
  Consider how your decisions and actions can influence your family and future generations.

*Modern Relevance:*

Rebekah's story has lasting relevance for believers today. It teaches us to trust God's guidance and make decisions based on faith, knowing that our actions can have a significant impact on the lives of our loved ones.

*Examples of Modern Relevance:*

1. Making Faith-Based Decisions: **People facing important decisions in their lives can be inspired by Rebekah's faith and trust in God's guidance.**
2. Influence on the Family: **Parents and family leaders can learn from Rebekah how their decisions can positively influence their children and future generations.**
3. Trust in God in Difficult Circumstances: **Rebekah's story reminds us that even in difficult circumstances, we can trust that God has a plan for us.**

*Importance in Theology:*

Rebekah is an important figure in Old Testament theology. His life and decisions played a crucial role in Israel's history and in the fulfillment of God's promises. Her story also highlights the importance of spiritual motherhood and a mother's influence on her children's lives.

*Reflection and Group Activity:*

- ❖ Reflect on a time when you've had to make a difficult decision and how God's guidance helped you in that process.
- ❖ Share as a group experiences of faith-based decisions and how they have impacted your life and the lives of others.
- ❖ Pray together for divine wisdom and guidance in the important decisions you face.

**Prayer:**

Lord, help us to follow your guidance and make decisions based on faith. Strengthen our confidence in your plans and allow our actions to positively influence our families and future generations. May our lives reflect your love and wisdom.

*Amen.*

## Grade Sheet:

**Questions to Reflect on and Answer:**

1. How can you apply Rebekah's obedience and trust in your daily life?

2. What important decisions are you facing, and how can you seek God's guidance in them?

3. How can you positively influence your family and future generations through your decisions?

4. What modern examples can you share that reflect Rebekah's faith and decisions?

**Summary of the Previous and Next Chapter:**
- **Previous Chapter:** Sarah - The Mother of Nations - Exploration of Sarah's life, her faith, and her role in God's promise.
- **Next Chapter:** Rachel and Leah - Sisterhood and Rivalry - Analysis of Rachel and Leah's life, their relationship with Jacob, and their importance in the formation of the twelve tribes of Israel.

---

*Chapter I. Patriarchal Period.*
## RACHEL AND LEAH
## – BROTHERHOOD AND RIVALRY –

Bible Text: Genesis 29-30.

*History and Context*:

Rachel and Leah were sisters and wives of Jacob, one of the patriarchs of Israel. Jacob, son of Isaac and grandson of Abraham, worked seven years to marry Rachel, Laban's youngest daughter, but was deceived and married to Leah, the eldest daughter, instead. Jacob worked another seven years to finally marry Rachel as well. This situation generated a dynamic of rivalry and competition between the sisters, especially in terms of motherhood.

*Challenges and Rivalry:*

The rivalry between Rachel and Leah centered on the ability to have children. Leah, who was less loved by Jacob, had several children quickly, while Rachel, whom Jacob loved most, was barren for many years. This situation generated tension and jealousy between the sisters. Rachel eventually gave birth to Joseph and Benjamin, while Leah was the mother of six of the twelve tribes of Israel.

*Faith and Reconciliation:*

Despite the rivalry, both women played crucial roles in Israel's history. Leah showed faith by trusting God to bless her with children despite not being preferred. Rachel, for her part, kept her faith and was eventually blessed with children who had a great impact on Israel's history. In the end, the rivalry morphed into a shared legacy that established the nation of Israel.

*Practical Applications and Reflections:*

- ❖ *Trust in God in Times of Difficulty:*
  *Reflect on how to trust God during times of rivalry and difficulty, as Rachel and Leah did.*
- ❖ *Overcoming Rivalry:*
  *Learn to overcome rivalry and seek reconciliation and peace, especially in family relationships.*
- ❖ *Value of Each Individual:*
  *Recognize the unique value and purpose of each person, just as God valued Rachel and Leah despite their differences.*

*Modern Relevance:*

The story of Rachel and Leah has significant relevance for believers today. It teaches us to trust God during times of difficulty and rivalry, and to seek reconciliation and peace in our relationships.

*Examples of Modern Relevance:*

1. Complex Family Relationships: **Complex family dynamics, such as sibling rivalries, can find guidance in Rachel and Leah's story, learning to trust God and seek reconciliation.**
2. Fertility and Hope: **Couples facing fertility challenges can find hope in Rachel's story, trusting that God has a perfect plan and timing.**
3. Embracing Diversity: **Rachel and Leah's story reminds us that each individual has a unique and valuable purpose in God's plan.**

*Importance in Theology:*

Rachel and Leah are central to Old Testament theology because of their role in the formation of the twelve tribes of Israel. Their stories highlight themes of love, rivalry, faith, and redemption, and show how God can work through complicated situations to fulfill His promises.

*Reflection and Group Activity:*

- ❖ Reflect on a time when you've experienced rivalry or jealousy and how you can seek reconciliation.
- ❖ Share as a group experiences of reconciliation and how God has worked in these situations.
- ❖ Pray together for healing and peace in family relationships and for those facing challenges similar to those of Rachel and Leah.

**Prayer:**

Lord, help us to trust you during times of rivalry and difficulty. Teach us to seek reconciliation and peace in our relationships. May our lives reflect your love and purpose, recognizing the unique value of each person.

*Amen.*

## Grade Sheet:

**Questions to Reflect on and Answer:**

1. How can you apply Rachel and Leah's trust in God in your daily life?

2. What rivalries or tensions do you need to overcome, and how can you seek reconciliation?

3. How can you recognize and value the unique purpose of each person in your life?

4. What modern examples can you share that reflect Rachel and Leah's story?

Summary of the Previous and Next Chapter:

- **Previous Chapter:** Rebekah - A Woman of Decision - Discusses Rebekah's life, her choice as Isaac's wife, and her role in the story of Jacob and Esau.
- **Next Chapter**: Miriam - Leadership and Worship - Explores the life of Miriam, Moses' sister, and her role in the exodus from Egypt and her leadership in Israel.

---

Chapter I. Patriarchal Period.

# CHAPTER II TERM OF JUDGES

## *MIRIAM*
## *– LEADERSHIP AND WORSHIP –*

Bible Text: Exodus 2:1-10; 15:20-21; Numbers 12

*History and Context:*

Miriam, the sister of Moses and Aaron, is a prominent figure in Israel's history. From the beginning, his care for his brother Moses, while still a baby on the Nile, shows his courage and wisdom. Later, Miriam becomes a key leader during the exodus from Egypt, standing out as a prophetess and worship leader.

*Challenges and Leadership:*

Miriam faced the challenge of leading in a male-dominated context. His role during the exodus, especially his victory song after the crossing of the

Red Sea, shows his influence and ability to inspire the people of Israel. However, she also faced moments of personal challenge, such as when she questioned Moses' authority and was punished with leprosy, only to be healed by her brother's intervention.

*Worship and Service:*

Miriam is remembered for her role in communal worship, leading women in dance and chant after the victory at the Red Sea. Her life reflects the importance of community worship and the vital role of women in the spiritual life of Israel.

*Practical Applications and Reflections:*

- ❖ Leadership in Worship:

    Reflect on the importance of leading in worship and how you can inspire others in their spiritual lives.

- ❖ Facing Personal Challenges:

    Learn to face and overcome personal challenges, trusting in God's mercy and forgiveness.

- ❖ Community Service:

    Consider how you can serve your community by guiding and supporting others in their faith.

*Modern Relevance:*

Miriam's story is relevant to believers today, teaching about the importance of spiritual leadership, community worship, and overcoming personal challenges. It shows us that women can play a significant role in spiritual and community life.

*Examples of Modern Relevance:*

1. Spiritual Leadership: **Women in spiritual leadership roles can find inspiration in Miriam, guiding and supporting their communities in worship and service.**
2. Overcoming Challenges: **Those facing personal challenges can learn from Miriam to rely on God's mercy and forgiveness to overcome their difficulties.**
3. Worship in Community: **Miriam's story reminds us of the importance of community worship and how it can strengthen our faith and unity.**

*Importance in Theology:*

Miriam is a significant figure in Old Testament theology, symbolizing God's spiritual leadership, worship, and mercy. Their lives and actions show how God can use women and men alike to lead His people and glorify His name.

*Reflection and Group Activity:*

- ❖ Reflect on times when you have led in worship and how you can follow Miriam's example.
- ❖ Share as a group experiences of overcoming personal challenges and how God's mercy has impacted your life.
- ❖ Pray together for opportunities for spiritual leadership, community worship, and service to others.

***Prayer:***

Lord, help us to follow Miriam's example in our spiritual leadership and worship. Strengthen our faith and our community, and give us the courage to face and overcome personal challenges. May our lives reflect your love and mercy, and may our actions be a testimony of your grace and power.

*Amen.*

## Grade Sheet:

**Questions to Reflect on and Answer:**

1. How can you apply Miriam's spiritual leadership in your daily life?

2. What personal challenges are you facing, and how can you rely on God's mercy to overcome them?

3. How can you inspire your community in worship and service, following Miriam's example?

4. What modern examples can you share that reflect Miriam's spiritual leadership and communal worship?

**Summary of the Previous and Next Chapter:**

- **Previous Chapter:** Rachel and Leah - Brotherhood and Rivalry - Explore the lives of Rachel and Leah, their relationship with Jacob, and the formation of the tribes of Israel.
- **Next Chapter:** Deborah - The Prophetess and Judge - Discusses Deborah's life, her leadership in Israel, and her role in the battle against Sisera.

---

Chapter II. Term of Judges.
# DEBORAH
## ~ THE PROPHETESS AND JUDGE ~

Bible Text: Judges 4-5.

*History and Context:*

Deborah was a prophetess and judge in Israel during the period of the judges, a time of turbulence and oppression for the people of Israel. She ruled under a palm tree, where people came to her to settle disputes and receive spiritual guidance. His leadership was crucial during the oppression of Jabin, king of Canaan, and his commander Sisera.

*Challenges and Leadership:*

Deborah faced the challenge of leading Israel at a time when female leadership was rare. Her courage and trust in God led her to summon Barak and lead Israel's army in a decisive victory over Sisera's forces. His victory song, along with Barak, is one of the oldest pieces of Hebrew poetry, celebrating Israel's liberation.

*Faith and Victory:*

Deborah's faith in God was the pillar of her leadership. their willingness to follow divine guidance and act boldly inspired all Israel to rise up against their oppressors. The victory of Deborah and Barak is a testimony to the power of faith and obedience to God.

*Practical Applications and Reflections:*

- ❖ *Leadership with Faith:*
  Reflect on the importance of leading in faith and how you can trust God to guide your decisions and actions.
- ❖ *Courage in Service:*
  Learn to show courage in your service to God and others, trusting in His power to overcome challenges.
- ❖ *Victory Celebration:*
  Consider how you can celebrate and thank God for the victories in your life by inspiring others with your testimony.

*Modern Relevance:*

Deborah's story is relevant to believers today, teaching about the importance of leadership with faith, courage in service, and celebrating victories. It shows us that God can use anyone, regardless of gender, to fulfill His purpose.

*Examples of Modern Relevance:*

1. Female Leadership: **Women in leadership roles can find inspiration in Deborah, relying on her faith to guide others and face challenges.**
2. Courage in Faith: **Those facing difficult situations can learn from Deborah's courage, trusting in God's power to overcome obstacles.**
3. Celebration and Testimony: **Deborah's story reminds us of the importance of celebrating God's victories in our lives and sharing our testimony with others.**

*Importance in Theology:*

Deborah is a significant figure in Old Testament theology, symbolizing leadership with faith and courage in service to God. Her life and actions show how God can use female leaders to bring deliverance and victory to His people.

*Reflection and Group Activity:*

- Reflect on times when you have led in faith and how you can follow Deborah's example.
- Share as a group experiences of courage in serving God and how they have impacted your life.
- Pray together for leadership opportunities with faith, courage in service, and celebration of victories in your lives and communities.

***Prayer:***

Lord, help us to follow Deborah's example in our leadership with faith and courage. Strengthen our trust in you and give us the courage to face and overcome challenges in our service to you and others. May our lives reflect your power and purpose, and may we celebrate and be grateful for your victories in our lives.

*Amen.*

## Grade Sheet:

**Questions to Reflect on and Answer:**

1. How can you apply Deborah's faith leadership in your daily life?

2. What challenges are you facing, and how can you show courage in your service to God and others?

3. How can you celebrate and thank God for the victories in your life by inspiring others with your testimony?

4. What modern examples can you share that reflect Deborah's faith leadership and courage?

_____
_____

*Summary of the Previous and Next Chapter:*

- Previous Chapter: Miriam - Leadership & Worship - Explore Miriam's life, her leadership during the exodus, and her role in communal worship.
- Next Chapter: Jael - The Brave Woman - Analyzes Jael's life, his decisive act of bravery, and his role in the victory over Sisera.

---

*Chapter II. Judges' Term*
# *JAEL*
## *– THE BRAVE WOMAN –*

Scripture: Judges 4:17-22; 5:24-27

*History and Context:*

Jael was the wife of Heber the Kenite, a nomadic group allied with the Canaanites. During the battle between the Israelites and the Canaanites, Sisera, the commander of the Canaanite army, sought refuge in Jael's tent after his defeat. Jael, showing surprising bravery, offered hospitality to Sisera only to then kill him in his sleep, ensuring a complete victory for Israel.

*Challenges and Courage:*

Jael faced the challenge of acting at a critical moment, knowing that his decision could have serious repercussions. Their courage and determination at that pivotal moment changed the course of Israel's history. Her action was celebrated in the Canto de Débora as an act of liberation and courage.

*Faith and Liberation:*

Jael's faith in God's purpose for Israel led her to act boldly and decisively. Their action shows that God can use anyone to accomplish His will and bring deliverance to His people.

*Practical Applications and Reflections:*

- ❖ Courage in critical moments:
  Reflect on the importance of acting boldly at critical moments and how you can trust God to guide your decisions.
- ❖ Faith and Obedience:
  Learn to act in faith and obedience, even when circumstances are difficult or dangerous.
- ❖ Deliverance and Divine Purpose:
  Consider how you can be an instrument of deliverance and fulfill God's purpose in your life and community.

*Modern Relevance:*

Jael's story is relevant to believers today, teaching about the importance of courage at critical moments, faith, and obedience to God. It shows us that God can use anyone, regardless of their situation, to fulfill His purpose and bring deliverance.

*Examples of Modern Relevance:*

1. Acts of Courage: **People facing critical decisions can find inspiration in Jael, trusting God to act boldly and decisively.**
2. Faith in Difficult Situations: **Those facing dangerous circumstances can learn from Jael's faith and obedience, trusting in the divine purpose for their lives.**
3. Deliverance and Purpose: **Jael's story reminds us of the importance of being instruments of deliverance and fulfilling God's purpose in our communities.**

*Importance in Theology:*

Jael is a significant figure in Old Testament theology, symbolizing courage at critical moments and faith in divine purpose. Their lives and actions show how God can use unexpected people to accomplish His will and bring deliverance to His people.

*Reflection and Group Activity:*

- Reflect on times when you've acted bravely and how you can follow Jael's lead.
- Share as a group experiences of faith and obedience in difficult situations and how they have impacted your life.

- Pray together for opportunities to be instruments of deliverance and fulfill God's purpose in your lives and communities.

*Prayer:*

Lord, help us to follow Jael's example in our courage and faith. It strengthens our resolve to act boldly in critical moments and to trust in your divine purpose. May our lives reflect your power and purpose, and may we be instruments of deliverance and blessing in our communities

*Amen.*

## Grade Sheet:

**Questions to Reflect on and Answer:**

1. How can you apply Deborah's faith leadership in your daily life?

2. What challenges are you facing, and how can you show courage in your service to God and others?

3. How can you celebrate and thank God for the victories in your life by inspiring others with your testimony?

_____
_____
_____

4. What modern examples can you share that reflect Deborah's faith leadership and courage?
_____
_____
_____

*Summary of the Previous and Next Chapter:*

**Previous Chapter:** Deborah - The Prophetess and Judge - Discusses Deborah's life, her leadership in Israel, and her role in the battle against Sisera.

**Next Chapter:** Ruth - Loyalty and Redemption - Explores Ruth's life, her relationship with Naomi, and her role in the genealogy of Jesus.

---

Chapter II. Term of Judges.
# RUTH
## – LOYALTY AND REDEMPTION –

Biblical Text: Book of Ruth.

*History and Context:*

Ruth, a Moabitess, is a prominent figure in the Bible for her loyalty and devotion to her mother-in-law, Naomi. After the death of her husband and two sons, Naomi decides to return to Bethlehem from Moab. Despite the difficulties, Ruth chooses to accompany Naomi, saying, "Your people will be my people, and your God my God." Her loyalty and determination lead her to a new beginning in Bethlehem.

*Challenges and Decisions:*

Ruth faced the challenge of being a foreigner in a new land. Her loyalty to Naomi and her willingness to work in the fields of Boaz, a relative of her late husband, show her character and determination. Eventually, her loyalty and diligence are rewarded when Boaz takes her as his wife, securing her place in Jesus' genealogy.

*Redemption and Divine Purpose:*

The story of Ruth is a story of redemption and divine purpose. Through her marriage to Boaz, Ruth becomes the great-grandmother of King David, and is thus in the genealogical line of Jesus. His life is a testimony to the power of redemption and divine providence.

*Practical Applications and Reflections:*

- ❖ Loyalty and Devotion:
  Reflect on the importance of loyalty and devotion in your relationships and how you can follow Ruth's example.
- ❖ Diligent Work:
  Learn to work diligently on all your tasks, trusting that God sees and rewards your efforts.
- ❖ Redemption and Purpose:
  Consider how you can trust God's redemptive purpose in your life, even in the midst of hardship

*Modern Relevance:*

The story of Ruth is relevant to believers today, teaching about the importance of loyalty, diligent work, and trust in God's redemptive purpose. It shows us that no matter our circumstances, God has a plan for our lives.

*Examples of Modern Relevance:*

1. Loyalty in Relationships: **People who face challenges in their relationships can find inspiration in Ruth, showing loyalty and devotion to their loved ones.**
2. Diligence at Work: **Those who seek to work diligently can learn from Ruth's work ethic, trusting that God sees and rewards their efforts.**
3. Confidence in God's Purpose: **The story of Ruth reminds us of the importance of trusting in God's redemptive purpose, even in the midst of difficulties.**

*Importance in Theology:*

Ruth is a significant figure in Old Testament theology, symbolizing loyalty, redemption, and divine purpose. Your life and actions show how God can use our decisions and efforts to fulfill His redemptive plan.

*Reflection and Group Activity:*

- Reflect on times when you have shown loyalty and devotion and how you can follow Ruth's example.
- Share as a group experiences of diligent work and how you have seen God's hand in your efforts.
- Pray together for opportunities to trust in God's redemptive purpose in your lives and communities.

***Prayer:***

**Lord,** help us to follow Ruth's example in our loyalty and devotion. It strengthens our resolve to work diligently and trust in your redemptive purpose in our lives. May our actions reflect your love and purpose, and may we be instruments of your redemption in our communities.

*Amen.*

## Grade Sheet:

### Questions to Reflect on and Answer:

1. How can you apply Ruth's loyalty and devotion in your daily relationships?
   _____
   _____

2. What tasks are you facing, and how can you work diligently, trusting in God's reward?
   _____
   _____

3. How can you trust God's redemptive purpose in your life, even in the midst of difficulties?
   _____
   _____

4. What modern examples can you share that reflect Ruth's loyalty, diligence, and redemption?

_____
_____
_____

Summary of the Previous and Next Chapter:

- **Previous Chapter:** Jael - The Brave Woman - Discusses Jael's life, his decisive act of bravery, and his role in the victory over Sisera.
- **Next Chapter:** Naomi - The Faithful Mother-in-Law - Explores Naomi's life, her relationship with Ruth, and her role in the story of redemption.

*Chapter II. Term of Judges.*
# NAOMI
## – THE FAITHFUL MOTHER-IN-LAW –

Biblical Text: Book of Ruth.

*History and Context:*

Naomi is a central figure in the book of Ruth. After the death of her husband and two sons in Moab, she decides to return to Bethlehem. Despite her bitterness and pain, Naomi shows deep fidelity and devotion to her family. His relationship with his daughter-in-law Ruth is a powerful example of love and family commitment.

*Challenges and Loyalty:*

Naomi faced the challenge of losing her family in a foreign land. Despite their pain, their faithfulness to Ruth and their willingness to return to Bethlehem show their strength and determination. Naomi also played a crucial role in Ruth's redemption, guiding and counseling her in her relationship with Boaz.

*Redemption and Providence:*

Naomi's life is a testimony of God's providence. Through her faithfulness and devotion, Naomi witnessed the redemption of Ruth and the restoration of her own life. His story shows us how God can bring redemption and purpose into our lives, even in the midst of grief and loss.

*Practical Applications and Reflections:*

- ❖ Faithfulness in Adversity:

  Reflect on the importance of maintaining fidelity and devotion in times of adversity.
- ❖ Guide and Counsel:

  Learn to be a guide and counselor to others, offering support and wisdom in difficult times.
- ❖ Trust in God's Providence:

  Consider how you can trust God's providence to bring redemption and purpose into your life.

*Modern Relevance:*

Naomi's story is relevant to believers today, teaching about the importance of faithfulness in adversity, guidance and counsel, and trust in God's providence. It shows us that God can use our lives and our relationships to fulfill His redemptive purpose.

*Examples of Modern Relevance:*

1. Faithfulness in Difficult Times: **People facing challenges can find inspiration in Naomi, maintaining their faithfulness and devotion in times of adversity.**
2. Guiding and Counseling Others: **Those who seek to be guides and counselors can learn from Naomi, offering support and wisdom to those around them.**
3. Trust in God's Providence: **Naomi's story reminds us of the importance of trusting in God's providence to bring redemption and purpose into our lives.**

*Importance in Theology:*

Naomi is a significant figure in Old Testament theology, symbolizing faithfulness in adversity and divine providence. Your life and actions show how God can use our relationships and our devotion to fulfill His redemptive plan.

*Reflection and Group Activity:*

- Reflect on times when you have shown faithfulness in adversity and how you can follow Naomi's example.
- Share as a group experiences of guiding and counseling others and how they have impacted your life.
- Pray together for opportunities to trust in God's providence and to be instruments of redemption in your communities.

**Prayer:**

Lord, thank you for Ana's example. Help me to be persistent in prayer and to trust in your promises. May my life be a testimony of your power and your faithfulness.

Amen.

## Grade Sheet:

**Questions to Reflect on and Answer:**

1. How can you apply Naomi's faithfulness in your daily life?

_____
_____

2. What challenges are you facing, and how can you offer guidance and counsel to others?

_____

3. How can you trust God's providence to bring redemption and purpose into your life?

4. What modern examples can you share that reflect Naomi's faithfulness and guidance?

Summary of the Previous and Next Chapter:

- **Previous Chapter:** Ruth - Loyalty and Redemption - Explore Ruth's life, her relationship with Naomi, and her role in the genealogy of Jesus.
- **Next Chapter:** Hannah - Prayer and Promise - Discusses Hannah's life, her plea for a son, and the birth of Samuel.

*Chapter II. Term of Judges.*

# CHAPTER III MONARCHICAL PERIOD

## *ANNA*
## *- PRAYER AND PROMISE -*

Bible Text: 1 Samuel 1-2

*History and Context:*

Hannah, one of Elkanah's two wives, is a central figure in the first book of Samuel. Despite being loved by her husband, Hannah suffered from being barren and was constantly provoked by Pennah, Elkanah's other wife, who had children. Sterility was considered a great misfortune in Israelite society, adding to Hannah's anguish.

*Challenges and Prayer:*

Hannah faced the challenge of barrenness and constant harassment from Peninnah. Her grief led her to cry out to God fervently at the tabernacle in Shiloh. He promised that if God would grant her a son, she would dedicate him to God's service for her entire life. God answered her prayer, and Hannah gave birth to Samuel, whom she dedicated to the Lord as she had promised.

*Promise and Delivery:*

True to her promise, Hannah took Samuel to the tabernacle after weaning him, giving him to Eli the priest to serve God. Her song of thanksgiving, known as the Song of Hannah, is a powerful hymn of praise and prophecy that reflects her deep faith and gratitude to God.

*Practical Applications and Reflections:*

- ❖ Fervent Prayer:
  Reflect on the importance of fervent prayer and how you can turn to God in times of distress and need.
- ❖ Promise Keeping:
  Learn to keep the promises made to God and others by following Hannah's example.
- ❖ Faith and Gratitude:
  Consider how you can show faith and gratitude to God for His answers to your prayers.

*Modern Relevance:*

Hannah's story is relevant to believers today, teaching about the importance of fervent prayer, the fulfillment of promises, and the expression of faith and thankfulness. It shows us that God hears our pleas and is faithful to respond to our needs.

*Examples of Modern Relevance:*

1. Persistent Prayer: **People facing challenges can find inspiration in Hannah by persisting in prayer and trusting in God's faithfulness.**
2. Keeping Promises: **Those who have made promises to God or others can learn from Hannah to fulfill with integrity and dedication.**
3. Faith and Gratitude: **Hannah's story reminds us of the importance of expressing our faith and gratitude to God for His answers and blessings.**

*Importance in Theology:*

Hannah is a significant figure in Old Testament theology, symbolizing fervent prayer, faith in God's promise, and thanksgiving for His blessings. His life and actions show how God hears and answers the prayers of his people, and how faith and dedication can have a lasting impact.

*Reflection and Group Activity:*

- Reflect on times when you have prayed fervently and how you can follow Hannah's example.
- Share as a group experiences of fulfilling promises and how they have impacted your life and the lives of others.
- Pray together for a spirit of fervent prayer, fulfillment of promises, and gratitude in your lives and communities.

***Prayer:***

Lord, help us to follow Hannah's example in our fervent prayer and fulfillment of promises. Strengthen our faith and gratitude, and allow our lives to be a witness of your faithfulness and love. May our actions reflect your grace and power, and may we be instruments of your blessing in our communities.

*Amen.*

## Grade Sheet:

**Questions to Reflect on and Answer:**

1. How can you apply Hannah's fervent prayer in your daily life?
___
___

2. What promises have you made to God or others, and how can you faithfully fulfill them?
___
___

3. How can you show faith and gratitude to God for His answers to your prayers?
___
___

4. What modern examples can you share that reflect Hannah's fervent prayer, fulfillment of promises, and gratitude?

*Summary of the Previous and Next Chapter:*

- **Previous Chapter:** Naomi - The Faithful Mother-in-Law - Explore Naomi's life, her relationship with Ruth, and her role in the story of redemption.
- **Next Chapter:** Abigail - Wise and Peaceful Woman - Analyzes Abigail's life, her peaceful intervention with David, and her wisdom in times of crisis.

---

*Chapter III. Monarchical period.*
## ABIGAIL
## – WISE AND PEACEFUL WOMAN –
Bible Text: 1 Samuel 25.

*History and Context:*

Abigail, wife of Nabal, is a prominent figure in 1 Samuel. Nabal was a rich but foolish and wicked man, while Abigail was intelligent and beautiful. When David and his men asked Nabal for food and drink, he flatly refused. David, enraged, decided to retaliate against Nabal and his household. However, Abigail, upon learning of the situation, acted quickly to prevent a disaster.

*Challenges and Wisdom:*

Abigail faced the challenge of having a foolish husband who put her family in danger. Showing great wisdom and diplomacy, he prepared a generous supply of food and drink and headed out to meet David. With humility and tact, Abigail pleaded with David not to shed innocent blood and reminded him that God had called him to be the future king of Israel. His peaceful and wise intervention prevented a bloody conflict and saved his family.

*Faith and Peace:*

Abigail's faith in God and her ability to act with wisdom and peace are notable examples. After Nabal's sudden death, David recognized her wisdom and took her as his wife. Abigail became one of David's wives, and her story shows how wisdom and peace can prevail in difficult situations.

*Practical Applications and Reflections:*

- ❖ *Wisdom in Adversity:*
  Reflect on the importance of acting wisely in difficult situations and how you can seek God's guidance in your decisions.
- ❖ *Peaceful Intervention:*
  Learn to intervene peacefully in conflicts, seeking solutions that honor God and bring peace.
- ❖ *Faith and Diplomacy:*
  Consider how you can combine your faith and diplomacy to solve problems and be an instrument of peace in your community.

*Modern Relevance:*

Abigail's story is relevant to believers today, teaching about the importance of wisdom in adversity, peaceful intervention, and the combination of faith and diplomacy. It shows us that God can use our wisdom and peaceful actions to avoid conflict and bring blessing.

*Examples of Modern Relevance:*

1. *Wisdom in Decision Making:* People facing difficult decisions can find inspiration in Abigail, acting wisely and seeking God's guidance.
2. *Conflict Intervention:* Those who intervene in conflict can learn from Abigail, seeking peaceful solutions and honoring God with their actions.
3. *Faith and Diplomacy:* Abigail's story reminds us of the importance of combining our faith and diplomacy to solve problems and bring peace to our communities.

*Importance in Theology:*

Abigail is a significant figure in Old Testament theology, symbolizing wisdom, peace, and faith in divine providence. His life and actions show how God can use our wisdom and diplomacy to avoid conflict and bring blessing to His people.

*Reflection and Group Activity:*

- Reflect on times when you've acted wisely in difficult situations and how you can follow Abigail's lead.
- Share as a group experiences of peaceful intervention in conflicts and how they have impacted your life and the lives of others.
- Pray together for opportunities to act wisely and be instruments of peace in your lives and communities.

***Prayer:***

Lord, help us to follow Abigail's example in our wisdom and peace. Strengthen our faith and guide our decisions, so that we may be instruments of your peace and blessing in our communities. May our actions reflect your love and purpose, and may we honor you in all that we do.

*Amen.*

## Grade Sheet:

**Questions to Reflect on and Answer:**

1. How can you apply Abigail's wisdom in your daily decisions?

    _____
    _____
    _____

2. What conflicts are you facing, and how can you intervene peacefully, seeking God's guidance?

    _____
    _____
    _____

3. How can you combine your faith and diplomacy to solve problems and be an instrument of peace?

    _____
    _____
    _____

4. What modern examples can you share that reflect Abigail's wisdom, peace, and faith?

    _____
    _____

*Summary of the Previous and Next Chapter:*

- **Previous Chapter:** Hannah - Prayer and Promise - Discusses Hannah's life, her plea for a son, and the birth of Samuel.
- **Next Chapter:** Bathsheba - From Sinner to Queen Mother - Explore Bathsheba's life, her relationship with King David, and her role as King Solomon's mother.

Chapter III. Monarchical period.
# BATHSHEBA
## – FROM SINNER TO QUEEN MOTHER –

Bible Text: 2 Samuel 11-12; 1 Kings 1-2

*History and Context:*

Bathsheba is a complex and significant figure in the Bible. Her story begins with her adulterous relationship with King David, an episode that has serious consequences. David, seeing her bathing, desires her and sends for her, even though she is the wife of Uriah, one of David's warriors. After Bathsheba becomes pregnant, David tries to cover up her sin and eventually orders Uriah's death on the battlefield.

*Challenges and Redemption:*

Bathsheba faces the challenge of falling victim to David's lust and the consequences of her sin. After Uriah's death, she becomes David's wife and Solomon's mother. The prophet Nathan confronts David, who repents, and although Bathsheba's first son dies, God blesses her marriage with the arrival of Solomon, who eventually becomes one of Israel's wisest and richest kings.

*From sinner to queen mother:*

Bathsheba's transformation from victim of adultery to queen mother is remarkable. Her influence as Solomon's mother and her role in securing the throne for her son shows her strength and wisdom. In 1 Kings 1-2, Bathsheba is a key figure in Solomon's succession to the throne, intervening decisively to secure his position.

*Practical Applications and Reflections:*

- ❖ *Redemption and Restoration:*
  Reflect on the possibility of redemption and restoration, regardless of past mistakes.
- ❖ *Positive Influence:*
  Learn to use your influence for good, supporting and guiding others toward their divine calls and purposes.
- ❖ *Strength and Wisdom:* Consider how you can show strength and wisdom in difficult situations, trusting in God's guidance.

*Modern Relevance:*

The story of Bathsheba is relevant to believers today, teaching about redemption and restoration, the positive use of influence, and the importance of strength and wisdom in difficult times. It shows us that God can transform our lives, no matter our past.

*Examples of Modern Relevance:*

1. Personal Redemption: **People who have made serious mistakes can find inspiration in Bathsheba, trusting that God offers redemption and restoration.**
2. Influence in the Family: **Those in positions of family influence can learn from Bathsheba to guide and support their loved ones toward their divine purposes.**
3. Strength in Adversity: **The story of Bathsheba reminds us of the importance of showing strength and wisdom in difficult times, trusting in God's guidance to overcome challenges.**

*Importance in Theology:*

Bathsheba is a significant figure in Old Testament theology, symbolizing redemption, restoration, and positive influence. His life and actions show how God can transform our lives and use us to fulfill His purpose, despite our past mistakes.

*Reflection and Group Activity:*

- Reflect on times when you have experienced redemption and restoration and how you can follow Bathsheba's example.
- Share as a group experiences of using your influence for good and how they have impacted your life and the lives of others.
- Pray together for strength and wisdom in difficult times and for opportunities to be instruments of redemption and restoration in your communities.

***Prayer:***

Lord, help us to follow Bathsheba's example in our quest for redemption and restoration. Strengthen our positive influence and wisdom in difficult times, and allow our lives to be a witness to your grace and transforming power. May our actions reflect your love and purpose, and may we be instruments of your redemption in our communities.

*Amen.*

## Grade Sheet:

### Questions to Reflect on and Answer:

1. How can you apply Bathsheba's redemption and restoration in your daily life?

2. What opportunities do you have to use your influence in a positive way in the lives of others?

3. How can you show strength and wisdom in difficult situations, trusting in God's guidance?

4. What modern examples can you share that reflect Bathsheba's redemption, positive influence, and strength?

Summary of the Previous and Next Chapter:

- **Previous Chapter:** Abigail - Wise and Peaceful Woman - Analyzes Abigail's life, her peaceful intervention with David, and her wisdom in times of crisis.
- **Next Chapter:** The Queen of Sheba - Wisdom and Wealth - Explore the Queen of Sheba's visit to Solomon, her search for wisdom, and the exchange of wealth.

---

Chapter III. Monarchical period.
# THE QUEEN OF SHEBA
## - WISDOM AND WEALTH -

Bible Text: 1 Kings 10:1-13; 2 Chronicles 9:1-12

*History and Context:*

The Queen of Sheba is a prominent figure who appears in the biblical account during the reign of Solomon. Hailing from a distant land, probably located in present-day Yemen or Ethiopia, the Queen of Sheba is known for her visit to Jerusalem to check the fame of Solomon's wisdom and wealth. He traveled with a large entourage and brought with him abundant riches, including gold, spices, and precious stones.

*Challenges and Pursuit of Wisdom:*

The Queen of Sheba faced the challenge of a long and arduous journey to seek the wisdom of Solomon. Her intellectual curiosity and desire to understand divine wisdom led her to interrogate Solomon with difficult questions. His visit was not only an exchange of material wealth, but also a recognition of the greatness of the God of Israel.

*Wisdom and Wealth:*

The queen was impressed by Solomon's wisdom and the greatness of his kingdom, recognizing that Israel's prosperity was a sign of God's blessing. His visit underscores the importance of divine wisdom and how it brings prosperity and recognition.

*Practical Applications and Reflections:*

- ❖ Wisdom Quest:
  Reflect on the importance of seeking divine wisdom and how you can apply this seeking in your daily life.
- ❖ Exchange of Blessings:
  Learn to share your blessings and recognize the source of all wisdom and prosperity in God.
- ❖ Recognition and Praise:
  Consider how you can recognize and praise God for the blessings and wisdom in your life.

*Modern Relevance:*

The story of the Queen of Sheba is relevant to believers today, teaching about the importance of seeking wisdom, exchanging blessings, and recognizing God's greatness. It shows us that divine wisdom brings prosperity and recognition.

*Examples of Modern Relevance:*

1. Intellectual and Spiritual Quest: **People who seek intellectual and spiritual growth can find inspiration in the Queen of Sheba, seeking divine wisdom in all areas of life.**
2. Sharing Blessings: **Those who have been materially blessed can learn from the Queen of Sheba to share in her riches and recognize the source of all blessings in God.**
3. Praise and Recognition: **The story of the Queen of Sheba reminds us of the importance of acknowledging and praising God for His wisdom and blessings in our lives.**

*Importance in Theology:*

The Queen of Sheba is a significant figure in Old Testament theology, symbolizing the search for divine wisdom and the recognition of God's greatness. His visit to Solomon and his praise of God show how divine wisdom brings prosperity and recognition, and how the nations can recognize God's blessing in his people.

*Reflection and Group Activity:*

- Reflect on times when you have sought divine wisdom and how you can follow the example of the Queen of Sheba.
- Share as a group experiences of exchanging blessings and how they have impacted your life and the lives of others.
- Pray together for a spirit of seeking wisdom, exchanging blessings, and acknowledging God's greatness in your lives and communities.

## Prayer:

Lord, help us to follow the example of the Queen of Sheba in our search for wisdom and recognition of your greatness. Strengthen our desire to share our blessings and to praise your name for your wisdom and provision. May our lives reflect your love and purpose, and may we be instruments of your blessing in our communities.

Amen.

## Grade Sheet:

### Questions to Reflect on and Answer:

1. How can you apply the Queen of Sheba's quest for wisdom in your daily life?

2. What blessings have you received, and how can you share them by acknowledging the source in God?

3. How can you recognize and praise God for His wisdom and blessings in your life?

4. What modern examples can you share that reflect the Queen of Sheba's quest for wisdom and recognition of God?

*Summary of the Previous and Next Chapter:*

- **Previous Chapter:** Bathsheba - From Sinner to Queen Mother - Explore Bathsheba's life, her relationship with King David, and her role as King Solomon's mother.
- **Next Chapter:** Rispa - Grief and Justice - Analyzes Rispa's life, her maternal devotion and her call to justice and dignity.

Chapter III. Monarchical period.
# RISPA
## ~ GRIEF AND JUSTICE ~

Bible Text: 2 Samuel 21:1-14

*History and Context:*

Rispa was a concubine of Saul and the mother of two of his sons, Harmoni and Mephibosheth. During a time of famine in Israel, King David discovered that the cause was an offense committed by Saul against the Gibeonites. To atone for this guilt, David handed over seven of Saul's descendants to the Gibeonites, who executed them and left their bodies exposed.

*Challenges and Maternal Devotion:*

Rispa, in an act of deep sorrow and devotion, remained watching over the bodies of her children from the beginning of the harvest until the rains came. Their brave act prevented birds and beasts from devouring the bodies, demonstrating their love and commitment to the dignity of their children.

### Justice and Dignity:

Rispa's act caught the attention of King David, who eventually ordered that the bones of Rispa's sons, along with those of Saul and Jonathan, be buried with dignity. This act of justice brought an end to the calamity in Israel and underscores the importance of justice and dignity.

### Practical Applications and Reflections:

- ❖ *Maternal Devotion:*
  Reflect on the importance of devotion and love in family relationships and how you can show this love in your daily life.
- ❖ *Seek Justice:*
  *Learn how to be a voice for justice and dignity in your community, following Rispa's example.*
- ❖ *Strength in Pain:*
  *Consider how you can show strength and devotion in times of pain and loss by trusting in God's justice.*

### Modern Relevance:

The story of Rispa is relevant to believers today, teaching about the importance of maternal devotion, the pursuit of justice, and strength in pain. It shows us that God values the dignity of each individual and hears the cry for justice.

*Examples of Modern Relevance:*

1. *Devotion and Family Love:* People facing family challenges can find inspiration in Rispa, showing devotion and love in their relationships.
2. *Fight for Justice:* Those who seek justice in their communities can learn from Rispa to be a voice for dignity and justice.
3. *Strength in Loss:* The story of Rispa reminds us of the importance of showing strength and devotion in times of grief and loss, trusting in God's justice.

*Importance in Theology:*

Rispa is a significant figure in Old Testament theology, symbolizing maternal devotion, justice, and dignity. Their life and actions show how God hears the cry for justice and values the dignity of each individual.

*Reflection and Group Activity:*

- Reflect on times when you have shown devotion and love in your family relationships and how you can follow Rispa's example.
- Share as a group experiences of seeking justice and how they have impacted your life and the lives of others.
- Pray together for strength and devotion in times of grief and loss and for opportunities to be a voice for justice and dignity in your communities.

***Prayer:***

Lord, help us to follow Rispa's example in our devotion and pursuit of justice. Strengthen our love and commitment in our family relationships, and give us the courage to be a voice for justice and dignity in our communities. May our lives reflect your love and justice, and may we be instruments of your grace and mercy.

*Amen.*

## Grade Sheet:

**Questions to Reflect on and Answer:**

1. How can you apply Rispa's maternal devotion in your daily relationships?

2. What injustices do you see in your community, and how can you be a voice for justice and dignity?

3. How can you show strength and devotion in times of pain and loss, trusting in God's justice?

4. What modern examples can you share that reflect Rispa's devotion, justice, and strength?

Summary of the Previous and Next Chapter:

- **Previous Chapter:** The Queen of Sheba - Wisdom and Wealth - Explore the Queen of Sheba's visit to Solomon, her search for wisdom, and the exchange of wealth.
- **Next Chapter:** Huldah - The Prophetess of King Josiah - Discusses the life of Huldah, her role in King Josiah's religious reform, and her importance as a prophetess in Israel.

Chapter III. Monarchical period.
# HULDAH
## – THE PROPHETESS OF KING JOSIAH –

Bible text: 2 Kings 22:14-20; 2 Chronicles 34:22-28

*History and Context:*

Huldah was a prophetess in Israel during the reign of King Josiah. His story is set in the context of the religious reformation carried out by Josiah. When the book of the Law was found in the temple, King Josiah sent his officials to consult Huldah to understand God's message and what actions they should take.

*Challenges and Prophecy:*

Huldah faced the challenge of interpreting and communicating God's will at a time of great importance to Israel. His message confirmed God's wrath against Judah for his idolatry, but it also included a promise of mercy to Josiah because of his repentance and devotion. Huldah's prophecy had a significant impact on Josiah's religious reform, leading to a return to pure worship and the elimination of idolatry.

*Faith and Obedience:*

Huldah's life reflects the importance of faith and obedience to God's word. Her willingness to serve as a messenger of God shows her devotion and commitment to divine truth. Huldah is one of the few women in the Bible who has an officially recognized prophetic role, highlighting her importance in Israel's history.

*Practical Applications and Reflections:*

- *Willingness to Serve:*
  Reflect on the importance of being willing to serve as God's messenger and how you can communicate His truth in your daily life.
- *Faith and Commitment:*
  Learn to live with faith and commitment, trusting in God's guidance and obeying His word.
- *Impact of Prophecy:*
  Consider how you can make a positive impact in your community by communicating God's truth and will.

*Modern Relevance:*

Huldah's story is relevant to believers today, teaching about willingness to serve, faith and commitment, and the positive impact of prophecy. It shows us that God can use anyone to communicate His truth and lead His people.

*Examples of Modern Relevance:*

1. *Communication of Truth:* **People who seek to be messengers of God can find inspiration in Huldah, communicating the truth and divine will in their lives.**
2. *Faith and Commitment:* **Those who wish to live with faith and commitment can learn from Huldah's life, trusting in God's guidance and obeying His word.**
3. *Positive Impact:* **Huldah's story reminds us of the importance of making a positive impact on our communities by communicating God's truth and leading others toward pure worship.**

*Importance in Theology:*

Huldah is a significant figure in Old Testament theology, symbolizing willingness to serve, faith, and commitment to divine truth. His life and actions show how God can use His messengers to guide His people and bring about spiritual reforms.

*Reflection and Group Activity:*

- Reflect on times when you have communicated God's truth and how you can follow Huldah's example.
- Share as a group experiences of faith and commitment and how they have impacted your life and the lives of others.
- Pray together for opportunities to serve as God's messengers and make a positive impact in your communities.

### Prayer:

Lord, help us to follow Huldah's example in our willingness to serve and communicate your truth. Strengthen our faith and commitment to you, and guide us to make a positive impact in our communities. May our lives reflect your love and purpose, and may we be instruments of your grace and mercy.

*Amen.*

## Grade Sheet:

### Questions to Reflect on and Answer:

1. How can you apply Huldah's willingness to serve in your daily life?

2. What challenges do you face in your faith and commitment, and how can you overcome them by trusting in God's guidance?

3. How can you make a positive impact on your community by communicating God's truth and will?

4. What modern examples can you share that reflect Huldah's willingness to serve, faith, and commitment?

Summary of the Previous and Next Chapter:

- **Previous Chapter:** Rispa - Grief and Justice - Analyzes Rispa's life, her maternal devotion and her call to justice and dignity.
- **Next Chapter:** Esther - Courage and Providence - Explore Esther's life, her courage in saving her people, and her trust in God's providence.

*Chapter III. Monarchical period.*

# CHAPTER IV PERIOD OF EXILE AND THE RETURN

## *ESTHER*
## *– COURAGE AND PROVIDENCE –*

Bible text: 2 Kings 22:14-20; 2 Chronicles 34:22-28

*History and Context:*

Esther, a young Jewish woman raised by her cousin Mordecai, became queen of Persia after gaining the favor of King Ahasuerus (Xerxes I). The story of Esther takes place during the period of Jewish exile in Persia. When Haman, a high official of the king, hatches a plot to exterminate all Jews in the kingdom, Mordecai urges Esther to use her position to save her people.

*Challenges and Courage:*

Esther faces the challenge of revealing her Jewish identity and risking her life to intervene with the king. She bravely stands before the king without being called, which was a potentially deadly act. Esther organizes a banquet where she reveals Haman's plot and her own identity as a Jew, getting the king to order Haman's execution and revoking the decree of extermination against the Jews.

*Divine Providence:*

The story of Esther is a clear example of divine providence. Through a series of seemingly fortuitous events, God positions Esther in a place of influence just at the time needed to save his people. Their story shows how God can use individuals in strategic positions to accomplish His purposes.

*Practical Applications and Reflections:*

- ❖ Courage in Adversity:
  Reflect on the importance of having courage in difficult situations and how you can trust God to guide your actions.
- ❖ Using Your Influence for Good:
  Learn to use your position and influence for the good of others, following Esther's example.
- ❖ Trust in God's Providence:
  Consider how you can trust God's providence in your life, knowing that He has a plan and purpose for every situation.

*Modern Relevance:*

The story of Esther is relevant to believers today, teaching about courage in adversity, using influence for good, and trusting in God's providence. It shows us that no matter our circumstances, God can use us to accomplish His purposes.

*Examples of Modern Relevance:*

1. Courage in Difficult Situations: **People facing difficult situations can find inspiration in Esther, showing courage and trust in God to guide their actions.**
2. Positive Use of Influence: **Those in positions of influence can learn from Esther to use her position for the good of others and to fulfill God's purposes.**
3. Trust in Divine Providence: **Esther's story reminds us of the importance of trusting in God's providence, knowing that He has a plan for our lives.**

*Importance in Theology:*

Esther is a significant figure in Old Testament theology, symbolizing courage, influence, and divine providence. Their lives and actions show how God can use individuals in strategic positions to fulfill His purposes and protect His people.

*Reflection and Group Activity:*

- Reflect on times when you have shown courage in difficult situations and how you can follow Esther's example.
- Share as a group experiences of using your influence for good and how they have impacted your life and the lives of others.
- Pray together for opportunities to show courage, use your influence for good, and trust in God's providence in your lives and communities.

**Prayer:**

Lord, help us to follow Esther's example in our courage and trust in your providence. Strengthen our faith and guide us to use our positions and influence for the good of others and to fulfill your purposes. May our lives reflect your love and purpose, and may we be instruments of your grace and mercy.

*Amen.*

## Grade Sheet:

**Questions to Reflect on and Answer:**

1. How can you apply Esther's courage in your daily situations?

2. What opportunities do you have to use your position and influence for the good of others?

3. How can you trust God's providence in your life, knowing that He has a plan and purpose for every situation?

4. What modern examples can you share that reflect Esther's courage, influence, and divine providence?

Summary of the Previous and Next Chapter:

- **Previous Chapter:** Huldah - The Prophetess of King Josiah - Discusses the life of Huldah, her role in King Josiah's religious reform, and her importance as a prophetess in Israel.
- **Next Chapter:** The Widow of Zarephath - Faith and Provision - Explore the life of the widow of Zarephath, her encounter with the prophet Elijah, and the miracle of divine provision.

---

Chapter IV. Period of Exile and Return.
# THE WIDOW OF ZAREPHATH
## – FAITH AND PROVISION –

Bible Text: 1 Kings 17:8-24

*History and Context:*

The widow of Zarephath lived in the region of Sidon during a time of great drought and famine. God sent the prophet Elijah to his house to be sustained. When he arrived, Elijah asked him for water and a piece of bread. The widow replied that she had only a handful of flour and a little oil, enough for one last meal for her and her son before they starved to death. Elijah asked him to trust God and to make him a small cake first, promising him that the flour and oil would not run out until the drought was over.

*Challenges and Faith:*

The widow faced the challenge of trusting the word of a stranger and the promise of a miracle in a time of dire need. Her act of faith in obeying Elijah resulted in miraculous provision that sustained her, her son, and the prophet throughout the drought. Later, when her son became ill and died, the widow's faith was again tested, but Elijah prayed and God raised the child from the dead.

Divine Provision:

The story of the widow of Zarephath highlights divine provision and the importance of faith in God. Through their obedience and faith, God miraculously provided for their needs and showed His power and care.

Practical Applications and Reflections:

- ❖ Faith in Times of Need:
  Ponder the importance of having faith in God during times of need and how you can trust His provision.
- ❖ Obedience and Trust:
  Learn to obey and trust God's promises, even when circumstances seem impossible.
- ❖ Miraculous Provision:
  Consider how God has miraculously provided in your life and how you can share these testimonies with others.

Modern Relevance:

The story of the widow of Zarephath is relevant to believers today, teaching about faith in times of need, obedience, and divine provision. It shows us that God is faithful to provide for our needs when we trust Him.

*Examples of Modern Relevance:*

1. Faith in Divine Provision: People facing financial or livelihood difficulties can find inspiration in the widow of Zarephath, trusting in God's provision.
2. Obedience to God: Those who seek to obey God's promises can learn from the widow of Zarephath, trusting that His word is faithful and true.
3. Provision Testimonies: The story of the widow of Zarephath reminds us of the importance of sharing testimonies of God's miraculous provision to strengthen the faith of others.

*Importance in Theology:*

The widow of Zarephath is a significant figure in Old Testament theology, symbolizing faith, obedience, and divine provision. His life and actions show how God can miraculously provide for our needs and how our faith in Him can be a powerful testimony.

*Reflection and Group Activity:*

- Reflect on times when you have trusted in God's provision and how you can follow the example of the widow of Zarephath.
- Share as a group experiences of divine obedience and provision and how they have impacted your life and the lives of others.
- Pray together for faith, obedience, and divine provision in your lives and communities.

***Prayer:***

Lord, help us to follow the example of the widow of Zarephath in our faith and obedience to your promises. Strengthen our confidence in your provision and guide us to share our testimonies of your miraculous provision. May our lives reflect your love and care, and may we be instruments of your grace and mercy in our communities.

*Amen.*

## Grade Sheet:

**Questions to Reflect on and Answer:**

1. How can you apply the faith of the widow of Zarephath in your daily situations of need?
   _____
   _____

2. What challenges are you facing, and how can you obey and trust God's promises?
   _____
   _____

3. How have you experienced God's miraculous provision in your life, and how can you share these testimonies with others?
   _____
   _____

4. What modern examples can you share that reflect the faith, obedience, and divine provision of the widow of Zarephath?

___

___

*Summary of the Previous and Next Chapter:*

- **Previous Chapter:** Esther - Courage and Providence - Explore Esther's life, her courage in saving her people, and her trust in God's providence.
- **Next Chapter:** The Shunammite Woman - Faith and Resurrection - Discusses the life of the Shunammite woman, her hospitality to Elisha, and the miracle of her son's resurrection.

*Chapter IV. Period of Exile and Return.*

## THE SHUNAMMITE WOMAN – FAITH AND RESURRECTION –

Bible Text: 2 Kings 4:8-37

*History and Context:*

The Shunammite woman is a notable figure in the ministry of the prophet Elisha. She and her husband were wealthy and lived in Shunem. Recognizing that Elisha was a man of God, she offered him hospitality every time he passed by her house, even building a small room for him. As a thank you for his generosity, Elisha prophesied that he would have a son, despite his advanced age.

*Challenges and Faith:*

The Shunammite woman faced the challenge of unbelief and grief. Although she initially struggled to believe Elisha's promise, she eventually gave birth to a son. Years later, the boy became ill and died suddenly. The

Shunammite woman showed unwavering faith in seeking Elisha, believing that God could resurrect her son. Elisha responded to his faith and the child was resurrected.

*Resurrection and Hope:*

The story of the Shunammite woman underscores the importance of hospitality, faith in God's promises, and hope in the resurrection. Their faith and persistence in seeking Elisha are powerful examples of trust in God's power to bring life back to what was dead.

*Practical Applications and Reflections:*

- ❖ Hospitality and Generosity:
  Reflect on the importance of hospitality and how you can open your home and heart to others.
- ❖ Faith in God's Promises:
  Learn to trust God's promises, even when circumstances seem impossible.
- ❖ Hope in the Resurrection:
  Consider how you can have hope in the resurrection and God's power to bring life and restoration.

*Modern Relevance:*

The story of the Shunammite woman is relevant to believers today, teaching about hospitality, faith in God's promises, and hope in the resurrection. It shows us that God is faithful to fulfill His promises and has the power to resurrect what is dead.

*Examples of Modern Relevance:*

1. Hospitality in the Community: **People who wish to practice hospitality can find inspiration in the Shunammite woman, opening their homes and hearts to others.**
2. Faith in Difficult Circumstances: **Those who face challenges can learn from the Shunammite woman to trust in God's promises, believing in His power to do the impossible.**
3. Hope in the Resurrection: **The story of the Shunammite woman reminds us of the importance of having hope in the resurrection and God's power to bring life and restoration.**

*Importance in Theology:*

The Shunammite woman is a significant figure in Old Testament theology, symbolizing hospitality, faith, and hope in the resurrection. His life and actions show how God can use our faith and hospitality to fulfill His promises and bring life back to what was dead.

*Reflection and Group Activity:*

- Reflect on times when you have practiced hospitality and how you can follow the example of the Shunammite woman.
- Share as a group experiences of faith in God's promises and how they have impacted your life and the lives of others.

- Pray together for hope in the resurrection and for opportunities to practice hospitality and faith in your lives and communities.

***Prayer:***

Lord, help us to follow the example of the Shunammite woman in our hospitality, faith, and hope in the resurrection. Strengthen our confidence in your promises and guide us to open our homes and hearts to others. May our lives reflect your love and power, and may we be instruments of your grace and restoration in our communities.

*Amen.*

## Grade Sheet:
### Questions to Reflect on and Answer:

1. How can you apply the hospitality of the Shunammite woman in your daily life?
   _____
   _____
   _____

2. What promises from God are you waiting for, and how can you trust His power to fulfill them?
   _____

3. How can you have hope in the resurrection and God's power to bring life and restoration?

4. What modern examples can you share that reflect the hospitality, faith, and hope of the Shunammite woman?

*Summary of the Previous and Next Chapter:*

- **Previous Chapter:** The Widow of Zarephath - Faith and Provision - Explore the life of the widow of Zarephath, her encounter with the prophet Elijah, and the miracle of divine provision.
- **Next Chapter:** Susanna – Justice and Purity – Discusses Susanna's life, her obedience to God's will, and her role in salvation history.

*Chapter IV. Period of Exile and Return.*

## *SUSANNA*
## *– JUSTICE AND PURITY –*

Bible Text: Daniel 13, Deuterocanonical

*History and Context:*

Susanna is a prominent figure in the book of Daniel, specifically in chapter 13, which is deuterocanonical. Susanna's story takes place during the Babylonian exile period. She was a beautiful and pious woman, married to Joachim, a wealthy and respected man. Two elder judges, full of lust, tried to force Susanna to commit adultery, but she refused to sin against God. In desperation, the elders falsely accused her of adultery, which sentenced her to death.

*Challenges and Justice:*

Susana faced the death threat due to the false accusations of the elders. However, she maintained her integrity and purity, trusting that God would vindicate her. As she was led to her execution, Susanna prayed to God, and her prayer was heard. Young Daniel intervened, separating the elders and examining them separately, which revealed their lies. Susanna was declared innocent and the elders received the punishment they had planned for her.

*Faith and Purity:*

Susanna's story underscores the importance of faith, purity, and justice. His willingness to face death rather than sin against God is a testament to his devotion and fortitude. Furthermore, God's intervention through Daniel demonstrates that divine justice prevails over human injustice.

*Practical Applications and Reflections:*
- Integrity and Purity:
  Reflect on the importance of maintaining integrity and purity, even in situations of extreme pressure.
- Faith in Divine Justice:
  Learn to trust in divine justice, believing that God will vindicate the righteous and punish the wicked.
- Courage in Adversity:
  Consider how you can show courage and faith when faced with false accusations or injustices.

*Modern Relevance:*

Susanna's story is relevant to believers today, teaching about integrity, faith in divine justice, and courage in adversity. It shows us that God is always with those who are faithful and pure, and that justice will prevail.

*Examples of Modern Relevance:*

1. Fighting Injustice: **People facing injustice can find inspiration in Susan, maintaining their integrity and trusting in divine justice.**
2. Defending Purity: **Those who value purity can learn from Susanna's example, resisting temptations and pressures to sin.**
3. Courage in Difficult Situations: **Susan's story reminds us of the importance of showing courage and faith in difficult situations, trusting that God will act on our behalf.**

*Importance in Theology:*

Susanna is a significant figure in the theology of the exile period, symbolizing integrity, faith in divine justice, and courage in adversity. His life and actions show how God vindicates the righteous and punishes the wicked, and how purity and faith are rewarded.

*Reflection and Group Activity:*

- Reflect on times when you have maintained your integrity and purity in difficult situations and how you can follow Susan's example.
- Share as a group experiences of facing injustice and trusting in divine justice.
- Pray together for courage and faith in difficult situations, and for the vindication of divine justice in your lives and communities.

**Prayer:**

Lord, help us to follow Susanna's example in our integrity and purity. Strengthen our faith in your divine justice and give us courage to face injustice with confidence in your vindication. May our lives reflect your love and grace, and may we be instruments of your justice and mercy in our communities.

*Amen.*

## Grade Sheet:

**Questions to Reflect on and Answer:**

1. How can you apply Susan's integrity and purity in your daily life?

2. What challenges do you face in your faith, and how can you trust divine justice?

3. How can you show courage and faith when faced with false accusations or injustices?

4. What modern examples can you share that reflect Susan's integrity, faith, and courage?

*Summary of the Previous and Next Chapter:*

- **Previous Chapter:** The Shunammite Woman - Faith and Resurrection - Discusses the life of the Shunammite woman, her hospitality to Elisha, and the miraculous resurrection of her
- **Next Chapter:** Judith - Courage and Strategy - Explore Judith's life, her bravery and strategy to save her people from the Assyrian invasion.

*Chapter IV. Period of Exile and Return*

# CHAPTER V
## PERIOD INTERTESTAMENTARY

## *JUDITH*
## *– VALUE AND STRATEGY –*

Biblical Text: Book of Judith, Deuterocanonical

*History and Context:*

Judith is a heroine of the Intertestamental period, whose story is found in the book of Judith, one of the deuterocanonical books. Judith, a wealthy and pious widow, lives in the city of Bethulia, which is under threat of invasion by Assyrian forces led by Holofernes, King Nebuchadnezzar's general. When her city's leaders are willing to surrender, Judith makes a courageous decision.

*Challenges and Strategy:*

Judith faced the challenge of an imminent invasion and the desperation of her people. Determined to save her city, she adorns herself with her best clothes and infiltrates the Assyrian camp. Using his intelligence and charm, he gains the trust of Holofernes and, when given the opportunity, beheads him. His act of bravery demoralises the Assyrian forces and saves his people.

*Courage and Faith:*

Judith showed great courage and faith in God. Her fervent prayer before her mission and her trust that God would lead her were crucial to her success. Her story is an example of how faith and courageous action can lead to liberation.

Practical Applications and Reflections:

- ❖ *Courage in Faith:*
  Reflect on the importance of acting with courage and trust in God, even in difficult situations.
- ❖ *Strategy and Wisdom:*
  Learn how to use wisdom and strategy in solving problems and challenges, following Judith's lead.
- ❖ *Active Faith:*
  Consider how you can put your faith into action to face and overcome adversity.

*Modern Relevance:*

Judith's story is relevant to believers today, teaching about the value in faith, strategy and wisdom, and the importance of active faith. It shows us that, with faith and courage, we can face and overcome great challenges.

*Examples of Modern Relevance:*

1. Courage in Adversity: People who face great challenges can find inspiration in Judith, trusting in God and acting with courage.
2. Wisdom in Problem Solving: Those who seek to solve difficult problems can learn from Judith's strategy and wisdom.
3. Faith in Action: Judith's story reminds us of the importance of putting our faith into action to overcome adversity.

*Importance in Theology:*

Judith is a significant figure in intertestamental theology, symbolizing courage in faith, strategy and wisdom, and active faith. His life and actions show how trust in God and courage can lead to deliverance and victory.

*Reflection and Group Activity:*

- Reflect on times when you have acted with courage and trust in God and how you can follow Judith's example.
- Share group experiences of using wisdom and strategy to solve problems and overcome challenges.
- Pray together for opportunities to put your faith into action, act with courage and wisdom, and face challenges with trust in God.

**Prayer:**

Lord, help us to follow Judith's example in our courageous faith and wisdom to face challenges. Strengthen our trust in you and guide us to act with courage and wisdom in our lives. May our actions reflect your power and grace, and may we be instruments of your deliverance and victory in our communities.

*Amen.*

## Grade Sheet:

**Questions to Reflect on and Answer:**

1. How can you apply Judith's courage and faith in your daily life?
_____
_____
_____

2. What challenges are you facing, and how can you use wisdom and strategy to overcome them?
_____
_____
_____

3. How can you put your faith into action to face and overcome adversity?
_____
_____
_____

4. What modern examples can you share that reflect Judith's courage, wisdom, and active faith?

Summary of the Previous and Next Chapter:

- **Previous Chapter:** Susana - Justice and Purity - Analyzes Susana's life, her defense of justice and her purity in the face of adversity.
- **Next Chapter:** Woman of the Maccabees - Courage and Faith - Explore the life of the mother of the Maccabees, her courage and faith in the face of the persecution and martyrdom of her children.

Chapter V. Intertestamental Period.

# *WOMAN OF THE MACCABEES*
## *- COURAGE AND FAITH -*

Bible Text: 2 Maccabees 7, Deuterocanonical

*History and Context:*

The wife of the Maccabees, whose name is not mentioned, is a central figure in the account of 2 Maccabees 7. During the reign of Antiochus IV Epiphanes, she and her seven sons were arrested and tortured for refusing to abandon their faith and abide by the king's laws, which forbade Jewish religious practices. As each child is tortured and killed, the mother encourages them to stand firm in their faith.

*Challenges and Courage:*

This woman faced the extreme challenge of seeing her children tortured and killed, one after another. Despite the unspeakable pain, he showed extraordinary courage, urging his children to remain faithful to God and the laws of their ancestors. Her unwavering faith and courage in the face of martyrdom make her a powerful symbol of devotion and bravery.

*Faith and Hope:*

The mother of the Maccabees showed deep faith and hope in the resurrection. He reminded his children that God would raise them to eternal life by their faithfulness. Her example of faith and hope in the face of death is an impressive testimony of spiritual strength and maternal love.

*Practical Applications and Reflections:*

- ❖ Courage in Faith:
  Reflect on the importance of maintaining faith and courage in situations of extreme adversity.
- ❖ *Hope in the Resurrection:*
  Learn to have hope in the resurrection and in the promise of eternal life, following the example of the mother of the Maccabees.
- ❖ *Spiritual Strength:*
  Consider how you can strengthen your spirit and faith to face difficult challenges with courage and hope.

*Modern Relevance:*

The story of the mother of the Maccabees is relevant to believers today, teaching about courage in faith, hope in the resurrection, and spiritual strength. It shows us that even in the most extreme situations, faith and hope can sustain us.

*Examples of Modern Relevance:*

1. Courage in the Face of Persecution: **People facing persecution for their faith can find inspiration in the mother of the Maccabees, maintaining their courage and faithfulness.**
2. Hope in Eternal Life: **Those facing difficult situations can learn from their hope in the resurrection and the promise of eternal life.**
3. Spiritual Strength: **The story of the mother of the Maccabees reminds us of the importance of strengthening our spirit and our faith to face challenges with courage and hope.**

*Importance in Theology:*

The mother of the Maccabees is a significant figure in intertestamental theology, symbolizing courage in faith, hope in the resurrection, and spiritual strength. His life and actions show how faith and hope can sustain us in the darkest of times.

*Reflection and Group Activity:*

- Reflect on times when you have shown courage in faith and how you can follow the example of the mother of the Maccabees.
- Share as a group experiences of hope in the resurrection and the promise of eternal life.
- Pray together for spiritual strength, courage in faith, and resurrection hope in your lives and communities.

**Prayer:**

Lord, help us to follow the example of the mother of the Maccabees in our courage in faith and in our hope in the resurrection. It strengthens our spirit and our faith to face challenges with courage and hope. May our lives reflect your love and grace, and may we be instruments of your mercy in our communities.

*Amen.*

## Grade Sheet:

**Questions to Reflect on and Answer:**

1. How can you apply the courage in the faith of the mother of the Maccabees in your daily life?

2. What challenges do you face, and how can you have hope in the resurrection and the promise of eternal life?

3. How can you strengthen your spirit and faith to face difficult challenges with courage and hope?

4. What modern examples can you share that reflect the courage, hope, and spiritual strength of the mother of Maccabees?

*Summary of the Previous and Next Chapter:*

- **Previous Chapter:** Judith - Courage and Strategy - Explore Judith's life, her bravery and strategy to save her people from the Assyrian invasion.

- **Next Chapter:** Mary - The Mother of Jesus - Discusses Mary's life, her role as the mother of Jesus, and her unwavering faith.

*Chapter V. Intertestamental Period.*

# CHAPTER VI PERIOD OF THE NEW TESTAMENT.

## *MARY*
## *– THE MOTHER OF JESUS –*

**Scripture:** Luke 1:26-38; 2:1-7; John 19:25-27

*History and Context:*

Mary, the mother of Jesus, is a central figure in Christianity and is revered for her faith and obedience to God. Mary was a young virgin living in Nazareth when the angel Gabriel appeared to her and announced that she would be the mother of the Savior. Despite the potential social and personal repercussions, Mary accepted God's will with humility and courage.

### Challenges and Faith:

Mary faced numerous challenges, from Joseph's unbelief to the journey to Bethlehem to Jesus' birth in a stable. His life was marked by faith and obedience to God, even when he didn't fully understand His plan. Throughout her life, from the flight into Egypt to the crucifixion of Jesus, Mary showed unwavering faith and deep devotion.

### Legacy and Devotion:

Mary was not only the biological mother of Jesus, but also a devoted follower of His ministry. He was present at several crucial moments in His life, including the wedding at Cana and the crucifixion. His legacy is one of unwavering faith, obedience, and devotion to God's will.

### Practical Applications and Reflections:

- ❖ Obedience to God:
  Ponder the importance of obeying God's will, even when you don't fully understand His plan.
- ❖ Faith in Difficult Times:
  Learn to maintain your faith in God in the midst of challenges and difficulties, following Mary's example.
- ❖ Devotion and Follow-up:
  Consider how you can be a devoted follower of Jesus in your daily life, demonstrating deep faith and devotion.

*Modern Relevance:*

Mary's story is relevant to believers today, teaching about obedience to God, faith in difficult times, and devotion and following of Jesus. It shows us that, with faith and obedience, we can fulfill God's will in our lives.

*Examples of Modern Relevance:*

1. Obedience in Everyday Life: **People who seek to obey God can find inspiration in Mary, accepting His will with humility and courage.**
2. Faith in Challenges: **Those facing challenges can learn from Mary's unwavering faith, trusting God in all circumstances.**
3. Devotion to Jesus: **Mary's story reminds us of the importance of being devoted followers of Jesus, actively participating in His ministry and work.**

*Importance in Theology:*

Mary is a significant figure in New Testament theology, symbolizing obedience to God, faith in difficult times, and devotion to Jesus. His life and actions show how faith and obedience to God's will can lead to the realization of His redemptive plan.

*Reflection and Group Activity:*

- Reflect on times when you have obeyed God's will and how you can follow Mary's example.
- Share as a group experiences of keeping the faith in the midst of challenges and difficulties.
- Pray together for greater obedience to God, faith in difficult times, and devotion to Jesus in your lives and communities.

## Prayer:

Lord, help us to follow Mary's example in our obedience to your will, our faith in difficult times, and our devotion to Jesus. Strengthen our trust in you and guide us to fulfill your plan in our lives. May our actions reflect your love and grace, and may we be instruments of your mercy and redemption in our communities.

*Amen.*

## Grade Sheet:

**Questions to Reflect on and Answer:**

1. How can you apply Mary's obedience to God in your daily life?
   _____
   _____

2. What challenges do you face, and how can you maintain your faith in God in those circumstances?
   _____
   _____

3. How can you demonstrate deep devotion and following to Jesus in your daily life?
   _____
   _____

4. What modern examples can you share that reflect Mary's obedience, faith, and devotion?
_____
_____

*Summary of the Previous and Next Chapter:*

- **Previous Chapter:** Woman of the Maccabees - Courage and Faith - Explore the life of the mother of the Maccabees, her courage and faith in the face of the persecution and martyrdom of her children.

- **Next Chapter:** Elizabeth - Mother of John the Baptist - Discusses Elizabeth's life, her faith, and her role as the mother of John the Baptist.

---

*Chapter VI. New Testament period.*
# *ELIZABETH*
## *- THE MOTHER OF JOHN THE BAPTIST -*

**Bible Text:** Luke 1

*History and Context:*

Elizabeth was a righteous and pious woman, a descendant of Aaron and wife of Zechariah the priest. She lived in a time when barrenness was seen as a disgrace, and although she and Zechariah were elderly, they had not had children. However, his faith and devotion to God remained steadfast.

*Challenges and Promise:*

Elizabeth faced the challenge of barrenness for many years, a burden she bore with dignity and faith. When Zechariah was serving in the temple, the angel Gabriel announced to him that Elizabeth would have a son, John, who would be the forerunner of the Messiah. Despite her advanced age, Elizabeth conceived and gave birth to John the Baptist, thus fulfilling God's promise.

*Faith and Gratitude:*

Elizabeth showed deep faith and immense gratitude to God for the blessing of a son. When Mary, the mother of Jesus, visited her, Elizabeth was filled with the Holy Spirit and proclaimed blessings upon Mary and her unborn child. His praise and gratitude to God are testimony to his devotion and faith.

*Practical Applications and Reflections:*

- Faith in God's Promise:
  Reflect on the importance of having faith in God's promises, even when they seem impossible.
- Gratitude in Blessings:
  Learn to express gratitude to God for His blessings, following Elizabeth's example.
- Mutual Support:
  Consider how you can support and bless others in their walk of faith, as Elizabeth did with Mary.

*Modern Relevance:*

Elizabeth's story is relevant to believers today, teaching about faith in God's promises, gratitude for His blessings, and mutual support in the faith community. It shows us that, with faith and gratitude, we can experience God's promises in our lives.

*Examples of Modern Relevance:*

1. Faith in God's Promises: **People who look forward to the fulfillment of God's promises can find inspiration in Elizabeth, trusting in His faithfulness.**
2. Gratitude in Daily Life: **Those who have received blessings can learn from Elizabeth's gratitude, expressing praise and gratitude to God.**
3. Support in the Community of Faith: **Elizabeth's story reminds us of the importance of mutual support in the community of faith, blessing and encouraging others in their walk with God.**

*Importance in Theology:*

Elizabeth is a significant figure in New Testament theology, symbolizing faith in God's promises, gratitude for His blessings, and mutual support in the community of faith. His life and actions show how faith and gratitude can lead to the fulfillment of God's promises.

*Reflection and Group Activity:*

- Reflect on times when you have trusted God's promises and how you can follow Elizabeth's example.
- Share as a group experiences of gratitude to God for His blessings.

- Pray together for greater faith in God's promises, gratitude in daily life, and mutual support in the faith community.

*Prayer:*

Lord, help us to follow Elizabeth's example in our faith in your promises, our gratitude for your blessings, and our support for one another in the community of faith. Strengthen our confidence in your faithfulness and guide us to bless and encourage others in their walk with you. May our lives reflect your love and grace, and may we be instruments of your mercy and blessing in our communities.

*Amen.*

### Grade Sheet:
**Questions to Reflect on and Answer:**

1. How can you apply Elizabeth's faith in God's promises in your daily life?

2. What blessings have you received, and how can you express gratitude to God for them?

3. How can you support and bless others in their walk of faith, following Elizabeth's example?

4. What modern examples can you share that reflect Elizabeth's faith, gratitude, and mutual support?

*Summary of the Previous and Next Chapter:*

- **Previous Chapter:** Mary - The Mother of Jesus - Discusses Mary's life, her role as the mother of Jesus, and her unwavering faith.
- **Next Chapter:** Anna, Prophetess - Hope and Devotion - Explore Hannah's life, her devotion in the temple, and her testimony of the coming of the Messiah.

*Chapter VI. New Testament period.*

# ANNA, THE PROPHETESS
# – HOPE AND DEVOTION –

**Bible Text:** Luke 2:36-38

*History and Context:*

Anna, the prophetess, is a remarkable figure in Luke's Gospel. Widowed from an early age, Hannah dedicated her life to God's service, spending her days and nights in the temple fasting and praying. At age 84, he had the privilege of seeing the baby Jesus when his parents took him to the temple to fulfill the Mosaic law.

*Challenges and Devotion:*

Ana faced the challenge of widowhood, a situation that often left women in a vulnerable position. However, instead of letting herself be dejected, Hannah dedicated her life to God, showing unwavering devotion. His steadfasting and prayer and temple service are testimony to his deep faith and hope in the redemption of Israel.

*Hope and Testimony:*

Hannah's prophecy and her recognition of Jesus as the Messiah reflect her unwavering hope and devotion to God. Seeing Jesus, Hannah thanked God and spoke of the child to all who were waiting for the redemption of Jerusalem. Their testimony is a reminder of the importance of hope and the proclamation of the message of salvation.

*Practical Applications and Reflections:*

- ❖ Constant Devotion:
  **Reflect on the importance of a life of constant devotion to God, following Hannah's example.**
- ❖ Hope in God's Promise:
  **Learn to keep hope in God's promises, even when the wait is long.**
- ❖ Active Testimony:
  **Consider how you can be an active witness of God's promises and salvation in your daily life.**

## Modern Relevance:

Hannah's story is relevant to believers today, teaching about constant devotion to God, hope in His promises, and active witness. It shows us that, with devotion and hope, we can be powerful witnesses to the message of salvation.

## Examples of Modern Relevance:

1. Devotion in Daily Life: **People who wish to deepen their relationship with God can find inspiration in Hannah by dedicating time to prayer and service.**
2. Hope in God's Promises: **Those who await the fulfillment of God's promises can learn from Hannah's unwavering hope.**
3. Testimony of Salvation: **Hannah's story reminds us of the importance of being active witnesses to the message of salvation, sharing God's hope and love with others.**

## Importance in Theology:

Hannah is a significant figure in New Testament theology, symbolizing constant devotion, hope in God's promises, and active witness. His life and actions show how faith and devotion can lead to a powerful witness to the message of salvation.

## Reflection and Group Activity:

- Reflect on times when you have shown consistent devotion to God and how you can follow Hannah's example.
- Share as a group experiences of hope in God's promises and how they have strengthened your faith.

- Pray together for greater devotion to God, hope in his promises, and active witness in your lives and communities.

**Prayer:**

Lord, help us to follow Hannah's example in our constant devotion to you, our hope in your promises, and our active witness to the message of salvation. Strengthen our faith and our dedication to your service, and lead us to be powerful witnesses of your love and grace. May our lives reflect your mercy and your salvation, and may we be instruments of your peace and hope in our communities.

*Amen.*

## Grade Sheet:

**Questions to Reflect on and Answer:**

1. How can you apply Hannah's constant devotion to God in your daily life?
   _____
   _____

2. What promises from God are you waiting for, and how can you keep hope in them?

3. How can you be an active witness to the message of salvation in your daily life?

4. What modern examples can you share that reflect Hannah's devotion, hope, and testimony?

*Summary of the Previous and Next Chapter:*

- **Previous Chapter:** Elizabeth - Mother of John the Baptist - Discusses Elizabeth's life, her faith, and her role as the mother of John the Baptist.
- **Next Chapter:** Martha - Serving with Hospitality - Explore Martha's life, her service to Jesus, and the importance of balancing service and worship.

*Chapter VI. New Testament period.*

# MARTHA
## – SERVE WITH HOSPITALITY –

**Scripture:** Luke 10:38-42; John 11:1-44

*History and Context:*

Martha, sister of Mary and Lazarus, is a prominent figure in the Gospels. She is known for her hospitality and diligent service. Martha lived in Bethany, a small village near Jerusalem, and her home was a place of refuge for Jesus and his disciples. In two significant events, Martha showed her love for Jesus and her willingness to serve Him.

*Challenges and Service:*

In Luke 10:38-42, Martha faces the challenge of balancing service with worship. As Mary sits at Jesus' feet to listen to his teachings, Martha is busy with preparations and is overwhelmed. Jesus reminds him of the importance of prioritizing his time with Him over worldly tasks.

In John 11:1-44, Martha shows deep faith during the illness and death of her brother Lazarus. She goes to meet Jesus and expresses her faith in his power to raise the dead. Your interaction with Jesus reveals your love, your faith, and your trust in Him.

*Service and Faith:*

Martha is an example of diligent service and faith in Jesus. Although she sometimes worries about the details of the service, her love and devotion to Jesus are evident. Their faith in the resurrection of Lazarus and their willingness to serve show their deep commitment to Jesus.

*Practical Applications and Reflections:*

- ❖ Balancing Service and Worship:
  Reflect on the importance of balancing service to God with time of worship and fellowship with Him.
- ❖ Faith in Times of Loss:
  Learn to keep faith in Jesus in times of loss and difficulty, following Martha's example.
- ❖ Service with Love:

Consider how you can serve God and others with love and dedication, showing hospitality and care.

*Modern Relevance:*

Martha's story is relevant to believers today, teaching about the balance between service and worship, faith in times of loss, and service with love. It shows us that, with faith and dedication, we can serve God and others in meaningful ways.

*Examples of Modern Relevance:*

1. Balance in Christian Life: **People who seek to balance their life of service with their time of worship can find inspiration in Martha, prioritizing their relationship with God.**
2. Faith in Adversity: **Those facing loss and difficulty can learn from Martha's faith, trusting in the power of Jesus.**
3. Loving Service: **Martha's story reminds us of the importance of serving with love and dedication, showing hospitality and care to others.**

*Importance in Theology:*

Martha is a significant figure in New Testament theology, symbolizing the balance between service and worship, faith in times of loss, and service with love. His life and actions show how faith and service to God can lead to a full and meaningful life.

*Reflection and Group Activity:*

- Reflect on times when you have balanced service to God with worship time and how you can follow Martha's example.
- Share as a group experiences of keeping the faith in times of loss and difficulty.

- Pray together for a balance between service and worship, faith in times of adversity, and loving service in your lives and communities.

*Prayer:*

Lord, help us to follow Martha's example in our service and worship of you. Strengthen our faith in times of loss and guide us to serve others with love and dedication. May our actions reflect your love and grace, and may we be instruments of your hospitality and care in our communities.

*Amen.*

## Grade Sheet:

**Questions to Reflect on and Answer:**

1. How can you apply the balance between service and Martha worship in your daily life?

2. What challenges do you face, and how can you maintain your faith in Jesus in times of loss?

3. How can you serve God and others with love and dedication, following Martha's example?

4. What modern examples can you share that reflect Martha's balance, faith, and loving service?

*Summary of the Previous and Next Chapter:*

- **Previous Chapter:** Hannah Prophetess - Hope and Devotion - Explore Hannah's life, her devotion in the temple, and her testimony of the coming of the Messiah.
- **Next Chapter:** Mary of Bethany - Devotion in Adoration - Analyzes the life of Mary of Bethany, her devotion to Jesus and her act of anointing.

*Chapter VI. New Testament period.*

# *MARY OF BETHANY*
# *- DEVOTION IN WORSHIP -*

**Bible Text:** John 12:1-8; Matthew 26:6-13

*History and Context:*

Mary of Bethany, sister of Martha and Lazarus, is known for her act of deep devotion to Jesus. In two Gospel accounts, Mary shows her love and adoration for Jesus in a remarkable way. In John 12, she anoints Jesus' feet with an expensive perfume and dries them with her hair. In Matthew 26, she anoints her head with the same perfume. These acts occurred in Bethany, in the house of Simon the leper, shortly before the crucifixion of Jesus.

*Challenges and Devotion:*

Mary faced critical challenge for her extravagant display of love and adoration. Some of the disciples, especially Judas, questioned the expense of expensive perfume. However, Jesus defended Mary, stating that her act of devotion would be remembered whenever the Gospel was preached.

*Love and Worship:*

Mary of Bethany is an example of sincere and loving devotion to Jesus. Their willingness to use such a valuable perfume to anoint Jesus shows their recognition of his divinity and their proximity to his suffering and impending death. Their act of worship transcends the cultural and social norms of their time.

*Practical Applications and Reflections:*

- ❖ Sincere Devotion and Worship:
  Reflect on the importance of showing sincere devotion and worship to Jesus, following Mary's example.
- ❖ Amor Sacrificial:
  Learn to demonstrate sacrificial love for Jesus and others, regardless of criticism or misunderstanding.
- ❖ Recognition of Divinity:
  Consider how you can recognize and honor the divinity of Jesus in your daily life by displaying acts of devotion and worship.

## Modern Relevance:

The story of Mary of Bethany is relevant to believers today, teaching about sincere devotion, sacrificial love, and recognition of the divinity of Jesus. It shows us that, with sincere devotion and worship, we can honor Jesus in meaningful ways.

## Examples of Modern Relevance:

1. Worship in Daily Life: **People who wish to deepen their relationship with Jesus can find inspiration in Mary, displaying acts of devotion and worship.**
2. Sacrificial Love: **Those who seek to demonstrate sacrificial love can learn from Mary's example, prioritizing their love for Jesus over cultural and social norms.**
3. Recognition of Divinity: **Mary's story reminds us of the importance of recognizing and honoring the divinity of Jesus, showing devotion and adoration in our daily lives.**

## Importance in Theology:

Mary of Bethany is a significant figure in New Testament theology, symbolizing sincere devotion, sacrificial love, and recognition of the divinity of Jesus. His life and actions show how sincere worship and devotion can lead to a deep and meaningful relationship with Jesus.

*Reflection and Group Activity:*

Reflect on times when you have shown sincere devotion and worship to Jesus and how you can follow Mary's example. Share as a group experiences of demonstrating sacrificial love for Jesus and others. Pray together for greater devotion and worship to Jesus, sacrificial love, and recognition of his divinity in your lives and communities.

**Prayer:**

Lord, help us to follow the example of Mary of Bethany in our devotion and adoration to you. Strengthen our sacrificial love and our recognition of your divinity. May our actions reflect your love and grace, and may we be instruments of your worship and devotion in our communities.

*Amen.*

## Grade Sheet:

**Questions to Reflect on and Answer:**

1. How can you apply Mary's sincere devotion and worship to Jesus in your daily life?

---
---
---

2. What challenges do you face, and how can you demonstrate sacrificial love to Jesus and others?

3. How can you recognize and honor the divinity of Jesus in your daily life, following Mary's example?

4. What modern examples can you share that reflect Mary's devotion, sacrificial love, and recognition of divinity?

*Summary of the Previous and Next Chapter:*

- **Previous Chapter:** Martha - Serving with Hospitality - Explore Martha's life, her service to Jesus, and the importance of balancing service and worship.
- **Next Chapter:** Mary Magdalene - Witness to the Resurrection - Discusses the life of Mary Magdalene, her testimony of Jesus' resurrection, and her devotion to her ministry.

*Chapter VI. New Testament period.*

# MARY MAGDALENE
## – WITNESS TO THE RESURRECTION –

**Scripture:** Luke 8:2-3; John 20:1-18

*History and Context:*

Mary Magdalene is one of the most prominent and well-known figures in the New Testament. She was a devoted follower of Jesus, from whom she had cast out seven demons (Luke 8:2). After her release, Mary Magdalene became one of Jesus' most faithful followers, supporting his ministry with her own resources.

*Challenges and Testimony:*

Mary Magdalene faced numerous challenges, from her deliverance from demons to her constant devotion to Jesus even in times of great danger. She was present at Jesus' crucifixion and was the first to see Him resurrected, becoming the first witness and messenger of the resurrection (John 20:1-18).

*Devotion and Transformation:*

The life of Mary Magdalene is a testimony of transformation and devotion. Her encounter with Jesus changed her life forever, and her devotion to Him was unwavering. Their witness to the resurrection is a fundamental pillar of the Christian message and shows their courage and faith.

*Practical Applications and Reflections:*

- ❖ Transformation in Christ:
  Reflect on the importance of personal transformation through an encounter with Jesus, following the example of Mary Magdalene.
- ❖ Devotion and Witness:
  Learn to be a faithful and devoted witness to Jesus, sharing the message of his resurrection and love with others.
- ❖ Courage in Faith:
  Consider how you can demonstrate courage in your faith, remaining faithful to Jesus even in times of difficulty.

*Modern Relevance:*

The story of Mary Magdalene is relevant to believers today, teaching about transformation in Christ, devotion and faithful witness, and courage in faith. It shows us that, with a personal encounter with Jesus, our lives can be transformed and we can be powerful witnesses of his love and resurrection.

*Examples of Modern Relevance:*

1. Personal Transformation: **People who seek transformation in their lives can find inspiration in Mary Magdalene, allowing Jesus to change their lives.**
2. Testimony of the Resurrection: **Those who wish to share the message of the resurrection can learn from the example of Mary Magdalene by being faithful and devoted witnesses.**

3. Courage in Faith: The story of Mary Magdalene reminds us of the importance of being courageous in our faith, remaining faithful to Jesus in all circumstances.

*Importance in Theology:*

Mary Magdalene is a significant figure in New Testament theology, symbolizing transformation in Christ, faithful devotion and witness, and courage in faith. His life and actions show how an encounter with Jesus can transform our lives and make us powerful witnesses of his love and resurrection.

*Reflection and Group Activity:*
- Reflect on times when you've experienced personal transformation through an encounter with Jesus and how you can follow Mary Magdalene's example.
- Share as a group experiences of being faithful and devoted witnesses of the message of the resurrection.
- Pray together for greater transformation in Christ, faithful devotion and witness, and courage in faith in your lives and communities.

**Prayer:**

Lord, help us to follow Mary Magdalene's example in our transformation into Christ, our faithful devotion and witness, and our courage in faith. Strengthen our relationship with you and guide us to be powerful witnesses of your love and resurrection. May our lives reflect your grace and your power, and may we be instruments of your salvation and hope in our communities.

*Amen.*

## Grade Sheet:

**Questions to Reflect on and Answer:**

1. How can you apply Mary Magdalene's personal transformation in your daily life?

2. What challenges do you face, and how can you be a faithful and devoted witness to the message of the resurrection?

3. How can you demonstrate courage in your faith, remaining faithful to Jesus even in times of difficulty?

4. What modern examples can you share that reflect Mary Magdalene's transformation, devotion, and courage?

*Summary of the Previous and Next Chapter:*

- **Previous Chapter:** Mary of Bethany - Devotion in Adoration - Discusses the life of Mary of Bethany, her devotion to Jesus, and her act of anointing.
- **Next Chapter:** The Woman with the Issue of Blood - Faith and Healing - Explores the life of the woman with the issue of blood, her faith, and her healing by Jesus.

## Chapter VI. New Testament period.

# THE WOMAN WITH THE ISSUE OF BLOOD
# – FAITH AND HEALING –

**Scripture:** Matthew 9:20-22; Mark 5:25-34

*History and Context:*

The woman with the issue of blood is a prominent figure in the Gospels, known for her faith and her pursuit of healing. For twelve years, this woman suffered constant bleeding, a condition that left her socially isolated and physically weakened. According to Jewish law, her condition made her ritually unclean, excluding her from religious and community life.

*Challenges and Faith:*

This woman faced numerous challenges, from social stigma to medical despair. He had spent everything he had on treatments without getting relief. However, her faith in Jesus was so strong that she believed that just touching the hem of his garment would she be healed. In the midst of a crowd, she came to Jesus and touched his garment, and instantly her bleeding stopped.

*Health and Catering:*

Jesus, perceiving that someone had touched his garment in faith, turned and sought it. When the woman confessed what she had done, Jesus praised her for her faith and said, "Daughter, your faith has healed you; go in peace and be healed of your affliction." Her healing was complete, both physically and spiritually, restoring her to the community and to a full life.

*Practical Applications and Reflections:*

- ❖ Persistent Fe:
  Reflect on the importance of persistent faith, even in the midst of prolonged challenges and despair.
- ❖ Health Search:
  Learn to seek healing in Jesus, trusting in His power to restore and heal.
- ❖ Complete Restoration:
  Consider how you can experience and testify about complete healing in Christ, both physical and spiritual.

*Modern Relevance:*

The story of the woman with the issue of blood is relevant to believers today, teaching about persistent faith, seeking healing, and full restoration in Christ. It shows us that, with faith in Jesus, we can experience his healing power and be restored to a full life.

*Examples of Modern Relevance:*

1. Faith in Adversity: **People facing prolonged challenges can find inspiration in this woman's persistent faith, trusting Jesus for their healing.**
2. Seeking Spiritual Healing: **Those seeking spiritual healing can learn from this woman's example by approaching Jesus in faith.**
3. Testimony of Restoration: **This woman's story reminds us of the importance of witnessing about the healing and restoration we find in Christ.**

*Importance in Theology:*

The woman with the issue of blood is a significant figure in New Testament theology, symbolizing persistent faith, the pursuit of healing, and complete restoration in Christ. Her life and actions show how faith in Jesus can lead to deep and transformative healing.

*Reflection and Group Activity:*

- Reflect on times when you have demonstrated persistent faith in the midst of prolonged challenges and how you can follow this woman's example.
- Share as a group experiences of seeking healing in Jesus and how you have experienced His healing power.
- Pray together for greater persistent faith, seeking healing, and witnessing restoration in your lives and communities.

**Prayer:**

Lord, help us to follow the example of the woman with the issue of blood in our persistent faith and our search for healing in you. Strengthen our confidence in your healing power and guide us to experience and testify of your full restoration. May our lives reflect your grace and power, and may we be instruments of your healing and hope in our communities.

*Amen.*

## Grade Sheet:

**Questions to Reflect on and Answer:**

1. How can you apply the woman's persistent faith with the flow of blood in your daily life?

2. What challenges do you face, and how can you seek healing in Jesus in these circumstances?

3. How can you experience and testify about healing and restoration in Christ in your daily life?

4. What modern examples can you share that reflect persistent faith, the pursuit of healing, and the woman's complete restoration with the issue of blood?

*Summary of the Previous and Next Chapter:*
- **Previous Chapter:** Mary Magdalene - Witness to the Resurrection - Discusses the life of Mary Magdalene, her testimony of Jesus' resurrection, and her devotion to her ministry.
- **Next Chapter:** The Syrophoenician Woman - Faith and Perseverance - Explores the life of the Syrophoenician woman, her faith and her perseverance in seeking healing for her daughter.

Chapter VI. New Testament period.
# THE SYROPHOENICIAN WOMAN
## – FAITH AND PERSEVERANCE –

**Scripture:** Matthew 15:21-28; Mark 7:24-30

*History and Context:*

The Syrophoenician woman, also known as the Canaanite woman, is a prominent figure in the Gospels of Matthew and Mark. She was not a Jew, but a pagan woman from the region of Tyre and Sidon. Her story centers on her encounter with Jesus as she desperately sought healing for her daughter, who was possessed by an unclean spirit.

*Challenges and Perseverance:*

This woman faced the challenge of getting closer to Jesus, despite being a foreigner in the Jewish community. His initial request was rejected by Jesus, who said that his mission was first for the children of Israel. However, the woman did not give up. Her faith and perseverance led her to persist in her plea, arguing that even dogs eat from the crumbs that fall from their masters' table. Admired for her faith, Jesus finally granted her request and healed her daughter.

*Faith and Humility:*

The faith of the Syrophoenician woman is an example of humility and perseverance. Despite obstacles and apparent refusals, she continued to seek Jesus' help with humility and trust in his power. Her story highlights the importance of unwavering faith and humility in the pursuit of God's grace and mercy.

*Practical Applications and Reflections:*

- ❖ Perseverance in Faith:
  Reflect on the importance of perseverance in faith, even when you face obstacles and rejections.
- ❖ Humility in Petition:
  Learn to approach God with humility and trust, knowing that He hears and answers our pleas.
- ❖ Faith in God's Grace:
  Consider how you can demonstrate unwavering faith in God's grace and mercy in your daily life.

*Modern Relevance:*

The story of the Syrophoenician woman is relevant to believers today, teaching about perseverance in faith, humility in petition, and faith in God's grace. It shows us that, with persevering and humble faith, we can receive God's grace and mercy in our lives.

*Examples of Modern Relevance:*

1. Perseverance in Prayer: **People facing persistent challenges can find inspiration in this woman's perseverance, continuing in prayer and faith.**
2. Humility in Seeking Help: **Those who seek God's help can learn from the humility of the Syrophoenician woman, approaching God with trust and humility.**
3. Faith in God's Grace: **This woman's story reminds us of the importance of having faith in God's grace and mercy, trusting in His response to our needs.**

*Importance in Theology:*

The Syrophoenician woman is a significant figure in New Testament theology, symbolizing perseverance in faith, humility in petition, and faith in God's grace. His life and actions show how an unwavering and humble faith can lead to the reception of divine grace.

*Reflection and Group Activity:*

- Reflect on times when you have demonstrated perseverance in faith and how you can follow the example of the Syrophoenician woman.
- Share as a group experiences of approaching God with humility and trust, and how you have experienced His grace and mercy.
- Pray together for greater perseverance in faith, humility in petition, and faith in God's grace in your lives and communities.

**Prayer:**

Lord, help us to follow the example of the Syrophoenician woman in our perseverance in faith and our humility in petition. Strengthen our trust in your grace and mercy and guide us to approach you with unwavering faith. May our lives reflect your love and power, and may we be instruments of your grace and hope in our communities.

*Amen.*

## Grade Sheet:

**Questions to Reflect on and Answer:**

1. How can you apply the perseverance in faith of the Syrophoenician woman in your daily life?

2. What challenges do you face, and how can you approach God with humility and confidence in those circumstances?

3. How can you demonstrate unwavering faith in God's grace and mercy in your daily life?

4. What modern examples can you share that reflect the perseverance, humility, and faith of the Syrophoenician woman?

*Summary of the Previous and Next Chapter:*

- **Previous Chapter:** The Woman with the Issue of Blood - Faith and Healing - Explores the life of the woman with the issue of blood, her faith, and her healing by Jesus.
- **Next Chapter:** The Samaritan Woman - Faith and Transformation - Analyzes the life of the Samaritan woman, her encounter with Jesus and her transformation.

### Chapter VI. New Testament period.
# THE SAMARITAN WOMAN
## – FAITH AND TRANSFORMATION –

**Bible Text:** John 4

*History and Context:*

The Samaritan woman is a prominent figure in the Gospel of John, known for her transformative encounter with Jesus at Jacob's well. Jesus, traveling from Judea to Galilee, stopped at Sychar, a city in Samaria, and found a Samaritan woman coming to draw water from the well. This encounter broke down cultural and religious barriers, as Jews and Samaritans did not treat each other.

*Challenges and Transformation:*

The Samaritan woman faced the challenge of her past life and her current situation, which included multiple marriages and a relationship outside of marriage. Despite this, Jesus approached it with compassion and offered "living water," a metaphor for eternal life and spiritual transformation. During their conversation, Jesus revealed his deep knowledge of his life and his identity as the Messiah.

*Faith and Testimony:*

Transformed by her encounter with Jesus, the Samaritan woman put down her pitcher and ran into the city to tell everyone about Jesus. His testimony led many Samaritans to believe in Jesus as the Savior of the world. Her life changed radically, becoming a fervent witness to the grace and truth of Jesus.

*Practical Applications and Reflections:*

- ❖ Spiritual Transformation:
  Reflect on the importance of spiritual transformation through an encounter with Jesus, following the example of the Samaritan woman.
- ❖ Active Testimony:
  Learn to share your faith and testimony with others, showing how Jesus has transformed your life.
- ❖ Breaking barriers:
  Consider how you can break down cultural and religious barriers to share Jesus' message with others.

*Modern Relevance:*

The story of the Samaritan woman is relevant to believers today, teaching about spiritual transformation, active witness, and the importance of breaking down barriers to share Jesus' message and that, in a personal encounter with Him, our lives can be transformed and we can be powerful witnesses to His love and grace.

*Examples of Modern Relevance:*

1. Personal Transformation: People seeking spiritual transformation can find inspiration in the Samaritan woman, allowing Jesus to change their lives.
2. Testimony of Faith: Those who wish to share their faith can learn from the example of the Samaritan woman, being active witnesses of Jesus' love and grace.
3. Breaking Cultural Barriers: This story reminds us of the importance of breaking cultural and religious barriers to share the Jesus message with

others.

## Importance in Theology:

The Samaritan woman is a significant figure in New Testament theology, symbolizing spiritual transformation, active witness, and the breaking down of cultural barriers. His life and actions show how an encounter with Jesus can transform our lives and make us powerful witnesses of his love and grace.

## Reflection and Group Activity:

- Reflect on times when you have experienced spiritual transformation through an encounter with Jesus and how you can follow the example of the Samaritan woman.
- Share as a group experiences of sharing your faith and testimony with others.
- Pray together for greater spiritual transformation, active witness, and the ability to break down cultural barriers to share the message of Jesus in your lives and communities.

**Prayer:**

Lord, help us to follow the example of the Samaritan woman in our spiritual transformation, our active witness, and our ability to break down barriers to share your message. Strengthen our relationship with you and guide us to be powerful witnesses of your love and grace. May our lives reflect your mercy and your power, and may we be instruments of your hope and salvation in our communities.

Amen.

*Women of the Bible: Strength, Faith and Legacy / José Arnaldo Lima Socarrás.*

## Grade Sheet:

**Questions to Reflect on and Answer:**

1. How can you apply the spiritual transformation of the Samaritan woman in your daily life?
   _____
   _____

2. What challenges do you face, and how can you share your faith and testimony with others?
   _____
   _____

3. How can you break down cultural and religious barriers to share Jesus' message with others?
   _____
   _____

4. What modern examples can you share that reflect the Samaritan woman's transformation, testimony, and breaking down barriers?
   _____
   _____

*Summary of the Previous and Next Chapter:*

- **Previous Chapter:** The Syrophoenician Woman - Faith and Perseverance - Explores the life of the Syrophoenician woman, her faith and her perseverance in seeking healing for her daughter.

- **Next Chapter:** Priscilla - Fellow Minister - Discusses Priscilla's life, her collaboration with Paul in the ministry, and her leadership in the early church.

---

*Chapter VI. New Testament period.*

# PRISCILLA
## – COLLABORATOR IN THE MINISTRY –

**Scripture:** Acts 18:2-3, 18-26; Romans 16:3-5; 1 Corinthians 16:19; 2 Timothy 4:19

*History and Context:*

Priscilla, also known as Prisca, is a prominent figure in the New Testament, known for her collaboration in ministry with her husband Aquila and the apostle Paul. Priscilla and Aquila were Jews expelled from Rome by Emperor Claudius and settled in Corinth, where they met Paul and joined his ministry.

*Challenges and Ministry:*

Priscilla and Aquila faced the challenge of being expelled from their home in Rome and settling in a new city. Despite these challenges, they dedicated themselves to ministry and opened their home to house a church in Ephesus. Priscilla played a crucial role in teaching and discipleship, instructing Apollos, an eloquent but limited knowledge of the Gospel, correcting it and teaching him the way of God more accurately.

*Collaboration and Leadership:*

Priscilla is an example of collaboration in ministry and leadership in the early church. Her willingness to work alongside her husband and Paul, as well as her leadership in the church in Ephesus, show her dedication and devotion to the gospel. His home was a place of hospitality and teaching, and his name is mentioned in several letters of Paul, highlighting his importance in the Christian community.

*Practical Applications and Reflections:*

- ❖ Collaboration in the Ministry:
  Reflect on the importance of collaboration in ministry, working together for the advancement of the Gospel.
- ❖ Leadership and Discipleship:
  Learn how to exercise leadership and discipleship in your community, following Priscilla's example.
- ❖ Hospitality & Service:
  Consider how you can open your home and serve others with hospitality and love, contributing to the growth of the church.

*Modern Relevance:*

Priscilla's story is relevant to believers today, teaching about collaboration in ministry, leadership and discipleship, and hospitality and service. It shows us that with dedication and devotion, we can contribute significantly to the advancement of the gospel and the growth of the church.

*Examples of Modern Relevance:*

1. Collaboration in Mission: **People seeking to collaborate in Christian mission can find inspiration in Priscilla, working together for the advancement of the Gospel.**
2. Leadership and Teaching: **Those who desire to exercise leadership and teach others can learn from Priscilla's example by dedicating themselves to discipleship and instruction in the faith.**

3. **Hospitality and Service:** Priscilla's story reminds us of the importance of hospitality and service, opening our homes and hearts to serve others.

*Importance in Theology:*

Priscilla is a significant figure in New Testament theology, symbolizing collaboration in ministry, leadership and discipleship, and hospitality and service. His life and actions show how dedication and devotion to the Gospel can lead to a lasting impact on the Christian community.

*Reflection and Group Activity:*

- Reflect on times when you have collaborated in ministry and how you can follow Priscilla's example.
- Share experiences of leadership and discipleship in your community as a group.
- Pray together for greater collaboration in ministry, leadership and teaching, and hospitality and service in your lives and communities.

**Prayer:**

Lord, help us to follow Priscilla's example in our collaboration in ministry, our leadership and discipleship, and our hospitality and service. Strengthen our dedication and devotion to the gospel and guide us to contribute to the growth of your church. May our lives reflect your love and grace, and may we be instruments of your mission and service in our communities.

*Amen.*

## Grade Sheet:

**Questions to Reflect on and Answer:**

1. How can you apply collaboration in Priscilla's Ministry in your daily life?

2. What challenges do you face, and how can you exercise leadership and discipleship in your community?

3. How can you open your home and serve others with hospitality and love, following Priscilla's example?

4. What modern examples can you share that reflect Priscilla's collaboration, leadership, and hospitality?

*Summary of the Previous and Next Chapter:*

- **Previous Chapter:** The Samaritan Woman - Faith and Transformation - Analyzes the life of the Samaritan woman, her encounter with Jesus, and her transformation.
- **Next Chapter:** Phoebe - The Helpful Deaconess - Explore Phoebe's life, her service in the church, and her role as a deaconess.

*Chapter VI. New Testament period.*
# PHOEBE
## – THE HELPFUL DEACONESS –

**Bible Text:** Romans 16:1-2

*History and Context:*

Phoebe is a prominent figure in Paul's letter to the Romans, where she is mentioned as a deaconess of the church in Cenchreae, a port near Corinth. Paul recommends her to the church in Rome, highlighting her service and asking them to receive her in the Lord in a dignified way and to help her in whatever she needs.

*Challenges and Service:*

Phoebe faced the challenge of being a woman in a position of leadership and service in the early church, a role that required courage and dedication. Her service as a deaconess involved a variety of responsibilities, from helping those in need to assisting in the administration of the church. His trip to Rome to deliver Paul's letter shows his commitment and willingness to serve the Christian community.

*Service and Support:*

Phoebe's name means "bright" or "pure," and her life reflected these qualities through her selfless service and dedication to the church. Her example of service is a reminder of the importance of helping others and being a light in our communities.

*Practical Applications and Reflections:*

- ❖ Selfless Service:
  Reflect on the importance of selfless service to others, following Phoebe's example.
- ❖ Leadership in the Church:
  Learn how to exercise leadership and service in your faith community, contributing to the growth and strengthening of the church.
- ❖ Hospitality and Support:
  Consider how you can show hospitality and help those in need in your daily life, being a light in your community.

*Modern Relevance:*

Phoebe's story is relevant to believers today, teaching about selfless service, leadership in the church, and hospitality and helping others. It shows us that, with dedication and willingness to serve, we can make a meaningful difference in our faith communities.

*Examples of Modern Relevance:*

1. Service in the Community: People who wish to serve their community can find inspiration in Phoebe, dedicating themselves to selfless service and helping those in need.
2. Leadership and Service: Those who seek to exercise leadership in the church can learn from Phoebe's example, contributing to the growth and strengthening of the faith community.
3. Hospitality and Help: Phoebe's story reminds us of the importance of showing hospitality and helping others, being a light in our communities.

*Importance in Theology:*

Phoebe is a significant figure in New Testament theology, symbolizing selfless service, leadership in the church, and hospitality and helping others. His life and actions show how service and dedication can lead to a lasting impact on the Christian community.

*Reflection and Group Activity:*

- Reflect on times when you have shown selfless service to others and how you can follow Phoebe's example.
- Share as a group experiences of exercising leadership and service in your faith community.
- Pray together for greater dedication to selfless service, church leadership, and hospitality and helping others in their lives and communities.

**Prayer:**

Lord, help us to follow Phoebe's example in our selfless service, our leadership in the church, and our hospitality and help to others. Strengthen our dedication and willingness to serve your community and guide us to be a light in our communities. May our lives reflect your love and grace, and may we be instruments of your service and hope in our communities.

*Amen.*

## Grade Sheet:
### Questions to Reflect on and Answer:

1. How can you apply Phoebe's selfless service in your daily life?

2. What challenges do you face, and how can you exercise leadership and service in your faith community?

3. How can you show hospitality and help others in your daily life, following Phoebe's example?

4. What modern examples can you share that reflect Phoebe's selfless service, leadership, and hospitality?

*Summary of the Previous and Next Chapter:*

- **Previous Chapter:** Priscilla - Collaborator in Ministry - Discusses Priscilla's life, her collaboration with Paul in ministry, and her leadership in the early church.
- **Next Chapter:** Lydia - First Convert in Europe - Explore Lydia's life, her conversion, and her hospitality to Paul and his companions.

## Chapter VI. New Testament period.

# LYDIA
# – FIRST CONVERTED IN EUROPE –

**Bible Text:** Acts 16:14-15

*History and Context:*

Lydia is a prominent figure in the book of Acts, known as the first convert to Christianity in Europe. She was a purple merchant from the city of Thyatira, a region known for its dyes and textiles. Lydia was a "God-fearer," a Gentile who worshipped the God of Israel, and her encounter with Paul and Silas in Philippi changed her life forever.

*Conversion and Hospitality:*

Lydia heard Paul preach by a river, and the Lord opened her heart to receive the gospel message. After being baptized along with her family, Lydia offered her home to Paul and his companions, showing remarkable hospitality and generosity. His home became a gathering place for the early Christians in Philippi.

*Faith and Service:*

Lidia's life is an example of faith and service. His willingness to open his home and support the missionaries shows his devotion and commitment to the Christian community. Lydia was not only a convert, but also a leader and servant in the nascent church in Europe.

*Practical Applications and Reflections:*

- ❖ Openness to the Gospel:
  Reflect on the importance of being open to the Gospel message and allowing God to open our hearts, following Lydia's example.
- ❖ Hospitality and Generosity:
  Learn to show hospitality and generosity to others, opening your home and supporting your faith community.
- ❖ Leadership and Service:
  Consider how you can exercise leadership and service in your community, contributing to the growth and strengthening of the church.

*Modern Relevance:*

Lydia's story is relevant to believers today, teaching about openness to the gospel, hospitality and generosity, and leadership and service in the church. It shows us that, with an open disposition and a generous heart, we can make a meaningful difference in our faith communities.

*Examples of Modern Relevance:*

1. Openness to God's Message: People who seek to be open to God's message can find inspiration in Lydia, allowing God to open their hearts.
2. Hospitality and Generosity: Those who wish to show hospitality and generosity can learn from Lydia's example, opening their homes and supporting their faith community.
3. Leadership in the Church: Lidia's story reminds us of the importance of leadership and service in the church, contributing to the growth and strengthening of the Christian community.

*Importance in Theology:*

Lydia is a significant figure in New Testament theology, symbolizing openness to the Gospel, hospitality and generosity, and leadership and service in the church. Their life and actions show how faith and a willingness to serve can lead to a lasting impact on the Christian community.

*Reflection and Group Activity:*

- Reflect on times when you have been open to the gospel message and how you can follow Lydia's example.
- Share group experiences of showing hospitality and generosity to others.
- Pray together for greater openness to the gospel, hospitality and generosity, and leadership and service in your lives and communities.

**Prayer:**

Lord, help us to follow Lydia's example in our openness to the gospel, our hospitality and generosity, and our leadership and service in the church. Strengthen our willingness to serve your community and lead us to be a light in our communities. May our lives reflect your love and grace, and may we be instruments of your message and hope in our communities.

*Amen.*

## Grade Sheet:
### Questions to Reflect on and Answer:

1. How can you apply openness to the Gospel of Lydia in your daily life?

2. What challenges do you face, and how can you show hospitality and generosity to others in those circumstances?

3. How can you exercise leadership and service in your community, following Lidia's example?

4. What modern examples can you share that reflect Lydia's openness to the gospel, hospitality and generosity, and leadership?

*Summary of the Previous and Next Chapter:*

- **Previous Chapter:** Phoebe - The Helpful Deaconess - Explore Phoebe's life, her service in the church, and her role as a deaconess.
- **Next Chapter:** Dorcas (Tabitha) - Life of Service and Resurrection - Discusses Dorcas' life, her service to those in need, and her resurrection by Peter.

Chapter VI. New Testament period.
# DORCAS (TABITE)
## – LIFE OF SERVICE AND RESURRECTION –

**Bible Text:** Acts 9:36-42

*History and Context:*

Dorcas, also known as Tabitha, is a prominent figure in the book of Acts, known for her life of service and charity. She lived in Joppa and was a beloved disciple in her community, known for her good works and acts of charity toward the poor and needy. The Bible describes her as a woman full of good works and almsgiving.

*Challenges and Miracle:*

Dorcas fell ill and died, causing great consternation in her community. The disciples in Joppa, when they heard that Peter was near at Lydda, called him. Peter came, and after praying, he said, "Tabitha, arise." Dorcas opened her eyes and sat down, and Peter presented her alive to believers and widows, leading many in Joppa to believe in the Lord.

*Service and Resurrection:*

Dorcas' life is an example of selfless service and dedication to others. His resurrection by Peter is a testimony to God's power and a confirmation of the importance of his service. Dorcas' story reminds us that our good works and acts of charity have a lasting impact and are valued by God.

*Practical Applications and Reflections:*

- ❖ Service Life:
  Reflect on the importance of living a life of service and charity, following Dorcas' example.
- ❖ Faith in the Power of God:
  Learn to have faith in God's power to work miracles and transform lives, as he did with Dorcas.
- ❖ Lasting Impact:
  Consider how your good works and acts of charity can have a lasting impact on your community and be a testimony of God's love.

*Modern Relevance:*

Dorcas' story is relevant to believers today, teaching about the life of service, faith in God's power, and the lasting impact of our good works. It shows us that with a life dedicated to service and charity, we can be instruments of God's grace and power in our communities.

*Examples of Modern Relevance:*

1. Selfless Service: **People who wish to live a life of service can find inspiration in Dorcas, dedicating themselves to good works and charity.**
2. Faith in Miracles: **Those who seek to experience God's power can learn from Dorcas' example, trusting in her ability to work miracles.**
3. Community Impact: **Dorcas' story reminds us of the importance of our good works and acts of charity, and how they can have a lasting impact on our communities.**

*Importance in Theology:*

Dorcas is a significant figure in New Testament theology, symbolizing the life of service, faith in God's power, and the lasting impact of our good works. His life and actions show how service and charity can lead to profound transformation and be a witness to God's love.

*Reflection and Group Activity:*

- Reflect on times when you have lived a life of service and charity and how you can follow Dorcas' example.
- Share as a group experiences of having faith in God's power to work miracles and transform lives.
- Pray together for a greater dedication to selfless service, faith in miracles, and a lasting impact on your communities.

**Prayer:**

Lord, help us to follow Dorcas' example in our life of service and charity. Strengthen our faith in your power to work miracles and guide us so that our good works will have a lasting impact on our communities. May our lives reflect your love and grace, and may we be instruments of your service and hope in our communities.

Amen.

## Grade Sheet:

**Questions to Reflect on and Answer:**

1. How can you apply Dorcas' service life in your daily life?

2. What challenges do you face, and how can you have faith in God's power to work miracles in those circumstances?

3. How can you ensure that your good works and acts of charity have a lasting impact on your community?

4. What modern examples can you share that reflect Dorcas' life of service, faith in miracles, and lasting impact?

*Summary of the Previous and Next Chapter:*

- **Previous Chapter:** Lydia - First Convert in Europe - Explore Lydia's life, her conversion, and her hospitality to Paul and his companions.
- **Next Chapter:** Joan - Follower and Benefactor of Jesus - Discusses Joan's life, her financial support of Jesus' ministry, and her testimony of his resurrection.

*Chapter VI. New Testament period.*

# JOAN
## – FOLLOWER AND BENEFACTOR OF JESUS –

**Scripture:** Luke 8:1-3; Luke 24:10

*History and Context:*

Joan is a figure mentioned in the Gospel of Luke, known for her financial and logistical support of Jesus' ministry. She was the wife of Chuza, the administrator of Herod Antipas, which placed her in a position of influence and resources. Joan used her position and assets to support Jesus and his disciples, traveling with them and providing the resources needed for their ministry.

*Challenges and Dedication:*

Joan faced the challenge of being a high-status woman who chose to follow Jesus, an itinerant rabbi, which could have brought criticism and personal risks. However, his dedication to Jesus and his ministry was steadfast. After Jesus' crucifixion, Joan was one of the women who discovered the empty tomb and brought the news of the resurrection to the disciples.

*Support and Testimony:*

Juana's life is an example of faithful support and testimony. Your willingness to use your resources for Jesus' ministry shows your commitment and love for the Lord. Their testimony of the resurrection is a reminder of their crucial role in the gospel and in the proclamation of the good news.

*Practical Applications and Reflections:*

- ❖ Support to the Ministry:
  Reflect on the importance of supporting Jesus' ministry with our resources and time, following Joan's example.
- ❖ Commitment and Dedication:
  Learn to show steadfast commitment and dedication as you follow Jesus, even when you face challenges and risks.
- ❖ Faithful Testimony:
  Consider how you can be a faithful witness to the gospel by sharing the good news of Jesus with others.

*Modern Relevance:*

Joan's story is relevant to believers today, teaching about ministry support, commitment and dedication, and faithful witness. It shows us that with dedication and willingness to use our resources for God's kingdom, we can make a significant difference in spreading the gospel.

*Examples of Modern Relevance:*

1. Ministry Support: **People who wish to support the ministry of Jesus can find inspiration in Joan, using her resources and time for the advancement of the Gospel.**
2. Commitment and Dedication: **Those who seek to show commitment and dedication can learn from Joan's example, following Jesus with firmness and love.**
3. Testimony of the Gospel: **Joan's story reminds us of the importance of being faithful witnesses of the Gospel, sharing the good news of Jesus with others.**

*Importance in Theology:*

Joan is a significant figure in New Testament theology, symbolizing support for ministry, commitment and dedication, and faithful witness. Their life and actions show how support and dedication to Jesus' ministry can lead to a lasting impact on the spread of the Gospel.

*Reflection and Group Activity:*

- Reflect on times when you have supported Jesus' ministry with your resources and time and how you can follow Joan's example.
- Share as a group experiences of showing commitment and dedication by following Jesus.
- Pray together for greater dedication to ministry support, commitment, and faithful witness in your lives and communities.

**Prayer:**

Lord, help us to follow Joan's example in our support of Jesus' ministry, our commitment and dedication, and our faithful witness to the Gospel. Strengthen our willingness to use our resources for your kingdom and guide us to be powerful witnesses of your love and grace. May our lives reflect your mercy and your power, and may we be instruments of your hope and salvation in our communities.

*Amen.*

*Women of the Bible: Strength, Faith and Legacy / José Arnaldo Lima Socarrás.*

## Grade Sheet:
**Questions to Reflect on and Answer:**

1. How can you apply support to Joan's ministry in your daily life?

2. What challenges do you face, and how can you show commitment and dedication by following Jesus in those circumstances?

3. How can you be a faithful witness to the Gospel, sharing the good news of Jesus with others?

4. What modern examples can you share that reflect Joan's support of ministry, commitment, and dedication?

*Summary of the Previous and Next Chapter:*

- **Previous Chapter:** Dorcas (Tabita) - Life of Service and Resurrection - Discusses Dorcas' life, her service to those in need, and her resurrection by Peter.
- **Next Chapter:** Rhoda - The Handmaid Who Listened to Peter - Explores Rhoda's life, her faith, and her role in the story of Peter's release from prison.

*Chapter VI. New Testament period.*

# RHODA
## – THE MAID WHO LISTENED TO PEDRO –

**Scripture:** Acts 12:12-15

*History and Context:*

Rhoda is a figure mentioned in the book of Acts, known for her role in the account of Peter's release from prison. She was a servant in the house of Mary, the mother of John Mark, where the disciples had gathered to pray for Peter, who had been imprisoned by Herod. His story stands out for his faith and his enthusiastic response to God's answer to his prayers.

*Challenges and Faith:*

Rhoda faced the challenge of being a maid in a situation of danger and uncertainty, as the church was under persecution. When Peter was miraculously freed from prison by an angel, Rhoda was the first to recognize his voice at the door. Her enthusiasm led her to leave Pedro outside as she ran to inform the others, who initially did not believe her story.

*Fe y Alegría:*

Rhoda's life is an example of faith and joy in God's answer to prayers. His ability to recognize Peter's voice and his joy at seeing God's answer to his prayers show a sincere faith and willingness to believe in miracles.

*Practical Applications and Reflections:*

- ❖ Faith in Prayer:
  Reflect on the importance of having faith in prayer, believing that God hears and answers, following Rhoda's example.
- ❖ Acknowledgment of God's Answers:
  Learn to be attentive to God's answers to our prayers and to recognize His work in our lives.
- ❖ Joy in Faith:
  Consider how you can experience and share joy in faith by celebrating God's answers to prayers.

*Modern Relevance:*

The story of Rhoda is relevant to believers today, teaching about faith in prayer, recognizing God's answers, and joy in faith. It shows us that, with sincere faith and a willingness to believe in miracles, we can experience the joy of seeing God's answers in our lives.

*Examples of Modern Relevance:*

1. Faith in the Efficacy of Prayer: People who wish to strengthen their faith in prayer can find inspiration in Rhoda, believing that God hears and responds.
2. Recognition of Miracles: Those who seek to recognize God's work in their lives can learn from Rhoda's example, being attentive to God's answers.
3. Celebration of Faith: Rhoda's story reminds us of the importance of celebrating faith and sharing the joy of God's answers with others.

*Importance in Theology:*

Rhoda is a significant figure in New Testament theology, symbolizing faith in prayer, recognition of God's answers, and joy in faith. His life and actions show how sincere faith and a willingness to believe in miracles can lead to a profound experience of God's work.

*Reflection and Group Activity:*

- Reflect on times when you have had faith in prayer and how you can follow Rhoda's example.
- Share as a group experiences of recognizing God's answers to prayers and how you have experienced His work in your life.
- Pray together for greater faith in prayer, recognition of God's answers, and joy in faith in your lives and communities.

**Prayer:**

Lord, help us to follow Rhoda's example in our faith in prayer and our willingness to recognize and celebrate your responses. Strengthen our confidence in your miraculous work and guide us to experience and share the joy of your love and your power in our lives. May our lives reflect your grace and mercy, and may we be instruments of your hope and healing in our communities.

*Amen.*

## Grade Sheet:

**Questions to Reflect on and Answer:**

1. How can you apply faith in the Rhoda Prayer in your daily life?

2. What challenges do you face, and how can you recognize God's answers to your prayers in those circumstances?

3. How can you experience and share joy in faith, celebrating God's answers to prayers?

4. What modern examples can you share that reflect Rhoda's faith in prayer, recognition of miracles, and joy?

*Summary of the Previous and Next Chapter:*

- **Previous Chapter:** Joan - Follower and Benefactor of Jesus - Discusses Joan's life, her financial support of Jesus' ministry, and her testimony of his resurrection.
- **Next Chapter:** The Woman with the Spirit of Sickness - Healing and Deliverance - Explores the life of women with the spirit of sickness, her healing by Jesus, and her deliverance.

## Chapter VI. New Testament period.
# *THE WOMAN WITH THE SPIRIT OF SICKNESS*
# *– HEALING AND DELIVERANCE –*

**Bible Text:** Luke 13:10-17

*History and Context:*

The woman with the spirit of sickness is a prominent figure in the Gospel of Luke, known for her healing and deliverance by Jesus. For eighteen years, this woman had been hunched over and couldn't straighten up. Her condition was caused by a spirit of illness, which left her physically weakened and socially marginalized.

*Challenges and Health:*

This woman faced numerous challenges, from her physical condition to social stigma. However, one Sabbath in the synagogue, Jesus saw her, called her, and said, "Woman, you are free from your disease." Then he laid his hands on her, and immediately straightened up and praised God. Her healing was immediate and complete, freeing her from her affliction and restoring her to a full life.

*Deliverance and Praise:*

This woman's life is an example of deliverance and praise. Her healing by Jesus not only restored her physical health, but also freed her from spiritual and social oppression. His immediate response was to praise God, showing his gratitude and faith.

*Practical Applications and Reflections:*

- ❖ Faith in God's Healing: Reflect on the importance of having faith in the healing and deliverance that God offers, following the example of the woman with the spirit of sickness.
- ❖ Gratitude and Praise: Learn to express gratitude and praise to God for His healing and deliverance, showing sincere faith and devotion.
- ❖ Complete Deliverance: Consider how you can experience and testify about complete deliverance in Christ, both physically and spiritually.

*Modern Relevance:*

The story of the woman with the spirit of sickness is relevant to believers today, teaching about faith in God's healing, gratitude and praise, and complete deliverance in Christ. It shows us that, with faith in Jesus, we can experience his healing power and be delivered from any affliction.

*Examples of Modern Relevance:*

1. Faith in Divine Healing: **People seeking healing can find inspiration in the woman with the spirit of sickness, trusting in the power of Jesus to heal.**

2. Gratitude for Blessings: **Those who have experienced healing and deliverance can learn from this woman's example, expressing gratitude and praise to God.**

3. Testimony of Deliverance: **This woman's story reminds us of the importance of testifying about the healing and deliverance we find in**

Christ.

*Importance in Theology:*

The woman with the spirit of sickness is a significant figure in New Testament theology, symbolizing faith in God's healing, gratitude and praise, and complete deliverance in Christ. Her life and actions show how faith in Jesus can lead to deep and transformative healing.

*Reflection and Group Activity:*

- Reflect on times when you have demonstrated faith in God's healing and deliverance and how you can follow this woman's example.
- Share as a group experiences of expressing gratitude and praise to God for their healing and deliverance.
- Pray together for greater faith in divine healing, gratitude for blessings, and a witness of deliverance in your lives and communities.

**Prayer:**

Lord, help us to follow the example of the woman in the spirit of sickness in our faith in your healing and deliverance. Strengthen our gratitude and praise for your blessings and guide us to experience and testify of your complete deliverance in our lives. May our lives reflect your grace and power, and may we be instruments of your healing and hope in our communities.

*Amen.*

## Grade Sheet:

**Questions to Reflect on and Answer:**

1. How can you apply faith in the healing and deliverance of women in the spirit of sickness in your daily life?

   _____
   _____
   _____

2. What challenges do you face, and how can you express gratitude and praise to God for His healing in those circumstances?

   _____
   _____
   _____

3. How can you experience and testify about complete deliverance in Christ in your daily life?

   _____
   _____
   _____

4. What modern examples can you share that reflect faith in divine healing, gratitude, and deliverance of women in the spirit of sickness?

   _____
   _____
   _____

*Summary of the Previous and Next Chapter:*

- **Previous Chapter:** Rhoda - The Handmaid Who Listened to Peter - Explore Rhoda's life, her faith, and her role in the story of Peter's release from prison.
- **Next Chapter** : The Adulterous Woman - Forgiveness and Restoration - Analyzes the life of the adulterous woman, her encounter with Jesus, and her restoration.

Chapter VI. New Testament period.

# THE ADULTEROUS WOMAN
## – FORGIVENESS AND RESTORATION –

**Bible Text:** John 8:1-11

*History and Context:*

The adulterous woman is a prominent figure in the Gospel of John, known for her encounter with Jesus that resulted in forgiveness and restoration. The scribes and Pharisees brought this woman, caught in adultery, before Jesus to test Him. According to the Mosaic law, she was to be stoned, but the religious leaders wanted to see how Jesus would handle the situation.

*Challenges and Forgiveness:*

This woman faced the challenge of being condemned to death for her sin, and her life was in the hands of those who sought to test Jesus. However, Jesus responded with wisdom and compassion. He said to them, "Whoever among you is without sin, let him be the first to throw a stone at it." One by one, the accusers left, and Jesus was left alone with the woman. He said to her: "Woman, where are they? None of them condemned you? ... Nor do I condemn you; go, and sin no more."

*Restoration and New Life:*

This woman's life is an example of forgiveness and restoration. Jesus not only saved her from physical condemnation, but also offered her a new life free of sin. Her encounter with Jesus changed her destiny, transforming her condemnation into an opportunity for a renewed life.

*Practical Applications and Reflections:*

- ❖ Divine Forgiveness:
  Reflect on the importance of accepting divine forgiveness and the restoration Jesus offers, following the example of the adulterous woman.
- ❖ Do Not Judge Others:
  Learn not to judge others, recognizing that we are all sinners and need God's grace.
- ❖ New Life in Christ:
  Consider how you can live a new life in Christ, leaving sin behind and embracing God's restoration and grace.

*Modern Relevance:*

The story of the adulterous woman is relevant to believers today, teaching about divine forgiveness, the importance of not judging others, and new life in Christ. It shows us that, with Jesus' forgiveness and restoration, we can leave sin behind and live a renewed life.

*Examples of Modern Relevance:*

1. Acceptance of Forgiveness: **People seeking forgiveness and restoration can find inspiration in the adulterous woman by accepting the grace of Jesus.**
2. Not Judging Others: **Those who struggle with judgment toward others can learn from Jesus' example, showing compassion and grace rather than condemnation.**

3. **Living in Grace:** The story of the adulterous woman reminds us of the importance of living in Christ's grace and restoration, leaving sin behind and embracing a new life.

*Importance in Theology:*

The adulterous woman is a significant figure in New Testament theology, symbolizing divine forgiveness, the importance of not judging others, and new life in Christ. His life and actions show how Jesus' forgiveness and restoration can transform our lives and offer us a new opportunity.

*Reflection and Group Activity:*

- Reflect on times when you have experienced Jesus' forgiveness and restoration and how you can follow the example of the adulterous woman.
- Share as a group experiences of not judging others and showing compassion and grace instead of condemnation.
- Pray together for greater acceptance of divine forgiveness, not judging others, and living in Christ's grace and restoration in your lives and communities.

**Prayer:**

Lord, help us to follow the example of the adulterous woman in accepting your forgiveness and restoration. Strengthen our ability not to judge others and to live in your grace and your new life. May our lives reflect your love and mercy, and may we be instruments of your forgiveness and hope in our communities.

*Amen.*

## Grade Sheet:

**Questions to Reflect on and Answer:**

1. How can you apply divine forgiveness and the restoration of the adulterous woman in your daily life?

2. What challenges do you face, and how can you learn not to judge others, showing compassion and grace in those circumstances?

3. How can you live a new life in Christ, leaving sin behind and embracing God's restoration and grace?

4. What modern examples can you share that reflect the adulterous woman's divine forgiveness, grace, and new life?

*Summary of the Previous and Next Chapter:*

- **Previous Chapter:** The Woman with the Spirit of Sickness - Healing and Deliverance - Explores the life of women with the spirit of sickness, her healing by Jesus, and her deliverance.
- **Next Chapter :** Susanna - Support and Service in Jesus' Ministry - Discusses Susan's life, support, and service in Jesus' ministry.

## Chapter VI. New Testament period.
# SUSANNA
## – SUPPORT AND SERVICE IN JESUS' MINISTRY –

**Bible Text:** Luke 8:3

*History and Context:*

Susanna is mentioned in Luke's Gospel as one of the women who supported and served in Jesus' ministry. Together with Mary Magdalene and Joan, Susanna used her resources to help Jesus and his disciples, showing her devotion and commitment to ministry. Although little is known about his life, his inclusion in this group highlights his importance and his role in supporting Jesus' ministry.

*Challenges and Service:*

Susana faced the challenge of being a woman who, in a patriarchal society, chose to follow and support an itinerant rabbi. Their willingness to use their resources for ministry shows their commitment and courage.

*Practical Applications and Reflections:*

- ❖ *Commitment in the Ministry:*

    Reflect on how you can support and serve in ministry in practical and engaged ways, following Susan's example.

- ❖ *Use of Resources:*

    Consider how you can use your resources and abilities to contribute to the advancement of God's kingdom.

- ❖ *Value of the Service:*

    Value the importance of service in the Christian life, recognizing that every act of support and help is meaningful.

*Modern Relevance:*

Susanna's example is relevant to believers today, as it demonstrates how commitment and support in ministry can have a lasting impact. Your willingness to serve and support Jesus inspires us to use our own resources to advance God's mission.

*Examples of Modern Relevance:*

1. Supporting Ministries: **Believers can follow Susan's example by supporting Christian ministries and causes financially and in other ways.**
2. Volunteer Service: **Susana's story motivates us to volunteer our time and skills in service to the church and community.**
3. Valuing Service: **The importance of service and support for God's work is a principle that remains relevant in the Christian life today.**

*Importance in Theology:*

Susanna represents the value of service and support in God's work, demonstrating that everyone, regardless of status, has a significant role in advancing God's kingdom. His example highlights the importance of selfless service in the Christian life.

*Reflection and Group Activity:*

- Reflect on how you can support and serve in your community and ministry, following Susan's example.

- Share ideas and experiences about using your resources to advance God's mission.
- Pray together for a heart willing to serve and support God's ministry in your lives.

*Prayer:*

Lord, we thank you for Susanna's example and her commitment to ministry. Help us follow their example of support and service, using our resources to advance your work. May our lives reflect a heart willing to serve and support your kingdom.

*Amen.*

## Grade Sheet:

**Questions to Reflect on and Answer:**

1. How can you apply Susanna's example in your daily life and in your service to God?
   _____
   _____
   _____

2. What resources do you have that you can use to support and serve in ministry?
   _____

3. How can you value and encourage service in the Christian community?

4. What modern examples do you know of that reflect support and selfless service in ministry?

*Summary of the Previous and Next Chapter:*

- **Previous Chapter:** The Adulterous Woman - Forgiveness and Restoration - Examines the story of the adulterous woman and her encounter with Jesus, focusing on forgiveness and new life.
- **Next Chapter :** Eunice and Lois - Transgenerational Faith - Discusses Eunice and Lois' faith and its impact on Timothy's life.

---

Chapter VI. New Testament period.

## *EUNICE AND LOIS*
## *– TRANSGENERATIONAL FAITH –*

**Bible Text:** 2 Timothy 1:5

*History and Context:*

Eunice and Lois are mentioned in Paul's letter to Timothy as examples of transgenerational faith. The faith of these women had a profound impact on the life of Timothy, who became a prominent leader in the early church. The influence of Timothy's mother Eunice and his grandmother Lois highlights the importance of faith inherited and passed down from generation to generation.

*Challenges and Faith:*

Eunice and Loida faced the challenge of maintaining their faith in a society that often did not value the role of women in the transmission of the faith. However, his commitment to God and his dedication to teaching Scripture to Timothy had a lasting impact on his life and ministry.

*Practical Applications and Reflections:*

- ❖ Transmission of the Faith:
  Reflect on the importance of passing on the faith to future generations, following the example of Eunice and Lois.
- ❖ Spiritual Education:
  Consider how you can educate and form young people in the faith, using your influence to guide them toward a Christian life.
- ❖ Value of Spiritual Inheritance:
  It values the importance of spiritual heritage in the Christian life and how faith can be a powerful legacy.

*Modern Relevance:*

The story of Eunice and Lois is relevant to believers today, as it emphasizes the importance of passing on the faith to the next generations. Their example shows us how influence and commitment to spiritual teaching can have a profound impact on the lives of young people.

*Examples of Modern Relevance:*

1. Family Christian Education: **Parents and grandparents can follow Eunice and Lois' example in educating and forming young people in the faith.**
2. Youth Ministries: **Eunice and Lois's influence motivates us to participate in ministries that educate and support young people in their spiritual growth.**
3. Spiritual Legacy: **The importance of leaving a spiritual legacy in our families and communities is a principle that is still relevant today.**

*Importance in Theology:*

Eunice and Lois represent the importance of transgenerational faith, demonstrating how faith can be passed down from generation to generation. His example highlights the lasting impact of spiritual education on the lives of believers.

*Reflection and Group Activity:*

- Reflect on how you can pass on your faith to future generations and educate young people in the faith.
- Share as a group experiences about the impact of inherited faith on your life and the lives of others.
- Pray together for a greater dedication to spiritual education and the transmission of the faith in your families and communities.

*Prayer:*

Lord, we thank you for the example of Eunice and Lois and their transgenerational faith. Help us to pass on our faith to future generations and to educate young people in your truth. May our lives reflect the lasting impact of inherited faith and commitment to your teaching.

*Amen.*

## Grade Sheet:

**Questions to Reflect on and Answer:**

1. How can you apply Eunice and Lois's example in passing on your faith to future generations?

2. What methods can you use to educate and form young people in the faith?

3. How can you value and promote the spiritual legacy in your family and community?

4. What modern examples do you know of that reflect the importance of transgenerational faith?

Summary of the Previous and Next Chapter:

- **Previous Chapter:** Susanna - Support and Service in Jesus' Ministry - Discusses Susan's life, her support and service in Jesus' ministry.
- **Next Chapter :** Junias - Apostle of Christ - Examines Junias' role as an apostle and his contribution to the ministry of the early church.

Chapter VI. New Testament period.
# JUNIAS
## – APOSTLE OF CHRIST –

**Bible Text:** Romans 16:7

*History and Context:*

Junias is mentioned in Paul's letter to the Romans as a prominent "apostle" in the early church. His inclusion in Paul's list of co-workers highlights his significant role and contribution to the ministry of the church. Although the text does not give extensive details about his life, Paul's recognition shows his status and contribution in apostolic work.

*Challenges and Ministry:*

Junias faced the challenge of being a woman in an apostolic role in a patriarchal society. His recognition by Paul underscores his worth and acceptance of his leadership in the Christian community.

*Practical Applications and Reflections:*

- ❖ Recognition of Vocations:
  Reflect on the importance of recognizing and valuing the calling and leadership of all believers, regardless of gender.
- ❖ Leadership in the Church:
  Consider how you can support and encourage women's leadership and ministry in the church.
- ❖ Assessment of the Apostolic Ministry:
  It values the role of apostolic ministry and how each member of the church can contribute to the advancement of God's kingdom.

*Modern Relevance:*

Junias' story is relevant to believers today in highlighting the importance of recognizing and valuing women's leadership in the church. Their example motivates us to support equality in ministry and to value the contributions of all members of the body of Christ.

*Examples of Modern Relevance:*

1. Female Leadership: **Junias' story encourages us to support and recognize women's leadership in the church and in ministry.**
2. Inclusion in Ministry: **The inclusion of Junias shows the importance of valuing the contributions of all believers in the work of the ministry.**

3. Vocation Assessment: **The story of Junias underscores the importance of recognizing God's call on the life of every believer.**

*Importance in Theology:*

Junias represents the value of women's leadership and contribution in ministry, highlighting the equality and importance of all members in the body of Christ. Her recognition by Paul demonstrates the acceptance and value of female apostolic ministry.

*Reflection and Group Activity:*

- Reflect on how you can support and recognize women's leadership in your church and community.
- Share experiences as a group about the importance of female leadership and its impact on ministry.
- Pray together for greater inclusion and appreciation of all members in the work of God's kingdom.

**Prayer:**

Lord, we thank you for Junias' example and her contribution to the ministry of the church. Help us to recognize and value the leadership of all believers, regardless of gender. May our lives reflect a spirit of inclusion and support in the work of God's kingdom.

*Amen.*

## Grade Sheet:

**Questions to Reflect on and Answer:**

1. How can you support and recognize women's leadership in church and ministry?

2. What role can you play in fostering equality in ministry and valuing the contributions of all members?

3. How can you value and support apostolic ministry in the church today?

4. What modern examples do you know of that reflect women's leadership and contribution in ministry?

*Summary of the Previous and Next Chapter:*

- **Previous Chapter:** Eunice and Lois - Transgenerational Faith - Discusses Eunice and Lois' faith and its impact on Timothy's life.
- **Next Chapter:** Conclusion and Final Thoughts - Closes the book with reflections and conclusions on the impact of women in the Bible and their relevance to the Christian life.

*Chapter VI. New Testament period.*

# FINAL CONCLUSIONS AND REFLECTIONS

*Final Thoughts:*

In this final chapter, the main themes and lessons learned throughout the book are summarized. It reflects on the impact and importance of women in the Bible and their relevance to believers today. The conclusion offers an overview of how these biblical examples can inspire and guide believers in their Christian lives.

*Practical Applications:*

1. Personal Inspiration: **Reflect on how the examples of women in the Bible can inspire you in your Christian and ministry life.**
2. Lesson Implementation: **Consider how you can apply the lessons learned in your daily life and in your service to God.**
3. Faith Strengthening: **Strengthen your faith by recognizing the value and impact of women in biblical history and in the life of the church.**

*Summary of Key Topics:*

- Examples of Faith and Courage: **A recap of the examples of women who demonstrated faith and courage in challenging situations.**
- Impact on the Christian Life: **Reflection on how these examples can influence modern Christian life.**
- Call to Ministry: **Inspiration to follow the call to ministry and service, following the example of women highlighted in the Bible.**

## *FINAL PRAYER:*

Lord, we thank You for the example of women in the Bible and for the lessons we have learned throughout their lives. Help us to apply these teachings in our daily lives and to follow their example of faith and service. May our lives reflect the impact of your grace and your call to serve you.

*Amen.*

# *APPENDICES*

## Appendix 1: Relevant Historical Documents

1. **Lineage of Jesus through Ruth and Mary**
   - This document traces the lineage of Jesus from Abraham to Mary, highlighting the crucial role of Ruth and Mary in God's redemptive plan. Ruth, a Moabite, becomes King David's great-grandmother through her marriage to Boaz, establishing a royal line that culminates in Jesus. Mary, mother of Jesus, closes this genealogical line, fulfilling the prophecies of the Old Testament.
2. **Timeline of Women of the Bible**
   - It provides a detailed timeline that places each woman in her historical context. It includes everything from Eve to the women of the New Testament, helping to understand their role and impact on the biblical narrative and how God used them to fulfill His divine purposes.

## Appendix 2: Key Bible Verse Lists

1. **Faith and Obedience Verses**
   - Luke 1:38: Mary accepts God's plan with obedience and faith.
   - Ruth 1:16-17: Ruth's loyalty to Naomi and her God.
2. **Verses of Courage and Courage**
   - Joshua 1:9: The exhortation to be courageous and strong, trusting in God's presence.
   - Esther 4:14: The call to courage to save his people.
3. **Service and Hospitality Verses**

- Romans 12:13: The practice of hospitality and sharing with those in need.
- 1 Peter 4:9: Hospitality without complaint.
4. **Verses of Wisdom and Peace**
    - James 1:5: The invitation to ask God for wisdom.
    - Matthew 5:9: The blessedness of peacemakers.

## Appendix 3: Diagrams and Tables

1. **Jesus Family Tree**
    - It shows the lineage from Abraham to Jesus, highlighting women such as Tamar, Rahab, Ruth, and Mary. It facilitates the understanding of how these women contribute to the fulfillment of the redemptive plan.
2. **Bible Women's Comparison Table**

**Comparison table of the characteristics of Biblical Women.**

| WOMAN | HISTORICAL CONTEXT | CHALLENGES | VIRTUES AND LESSONS |
|---|---|---|---|
| Abigail | 1 Samuel 25 | Wisdom and Reconciliation | Wisdom and Peace |
| Anna | 1 Samuel 1-2 | Infertility and prayer | Devotion and faith |
| Deborah | Judges 4-5 | War and Trial | Courage and justice |
| Elizabeth | Luke 1:5-25; 57-66 | Promise and Obedience | Faith and Divine Fulfillment |
| Ester | Book of Esther | Persecution and Liberation | Courage and providence |
| Eve | Genesis 2-3 | Temptation and Fall | Need for Obedience and Grace |
| Phoebe | Romans 16:1-2 | Diakonia and leadership | Help and dedication |
| Lydia | Acts 16:14-15 | Conversion and hospitality | Faith and generosity |
| Mary Mother of Jesus | Luke 1-2; John 19 | Motherhood of Jesus | Obedience and humility |
| Marten | Luke 10:38-42; John 11:1-44 | Service and faith | Hospitality and balance |
| Mary of Bethany | John 12:1-8; Matthew 26:6-13 | Devotion to Jesus | Adoration and total surrender |
| Miriam | Exodus 2:15; Numbers 12 | Leadership and Worship | Leadership and Service |

Women of the Bible: Strength, Faith and Legacy / José Arnaldo Lima Socarrás.

| | | | |
|---|---|---|---|
| **Woman with Blood Discharge** | Matthew 9:20-22; Mark 5:25-34 | Perseverance and healing | Faith and perseverance |
| **Samaritan Woman** | John 4 | Revelation of Jesus | Witness and evangelization |
| **Canaanite Woman** | Matthew 15:21-28 | Perseverance in Faith | Insistence and reward |
| **Mary Magdalene** | Luke 8:2-3; John 20:1-18 | Testimony of the Resurrection | Devotion and Faithfulness |
| **Priscilla** | Acts 18:2-3; Romans 16:3-5 | Collaboration in the Ministry | Service and education |
| **Raquel and Leah** | Genesis 29-35 | Rivalry and motherhood | Perseverance and reconciliation |
| **Cardigan** | Genesis 24-27 | Family decisions | Obedience and Discernment |
| **Ruth** | Book of Ruth | Widowhood and redemption | Loyalty and redemption |
| **Sara** | Genesis 17-21 | Sterility and waiting | Faith in God's Promises |
| **Widow of Zarephath** | 1 Kings 17:8-24 | Faith in Times of Need | Divine Trust and Provision |
| **Widow with the Two Whites** | Mark 12:41-44; Luke 21:1-4 | Extreme generosity | Total Sacrifice and Faith |

By the Author. 2024

# *NOTES*

1. **References to the Women of the Bible:**

   - Eve: Genesis 2:18-23; Genesis 3:1-6; Genesis 3:20
   - Sarah: Genesis 17-21
   - Rebekah: Genesis 24-27
   - Rachel and Leah: Genesis 29-30
   - Miriam: Exodus 2:1-10; Exodus 15:20-21; Figure 12
   - Deborah: Judges 4-5
   - Jael: Judges 4:17-22; 5:24-27
   - Ruth: Book of Ruth
   - Naomi: The Book of Ruth
   - Ana: 1 Samuel 1-2
   - Abigail: 1 Samuel 25
   - Bathsheba: 2 Samuel 11-12; 1 Kings 1-2
   - The Queen of Sheba: 1 Kings 10:1-13; 2 Chronicles 9:1-12
   - Rispa: 2 Samuel 21: 1-14
   - Huldah: 2 Kings 22:14-20; 2 Chronicles 34:22-28
   - Esther: Book of Esther
   - The Widow of Zarephath: 1 Kings 17:8-24
   - The Shunammite Woman: 2 Kings 4:8-37
   - Susanna: Daniel 13, Deuterocanonical
   - Judith: Book of Judith, Deuterocanonical
   - Woman of the Cambees: 2 Maccabees 7, Deuterocanonical
   - Mary (Mother of Jesus): Luke 1:26-38; 2: 1-7; John 19:25-27
   - Elizabeth: Luke 1:5-25; Luke 1:57-66
   - Hannah Prophetess: Luke 2:36-38
   - Martha: Luke 10:38-42; John 11:1-44
   - Mary of Bethany: John 12:1-8; Matthew 26:6-13
   - Mary Magdalene: Luke 8:2-3; John 20:1-18
   - The Woman with the Issue of Blood: Matthew 9:20-22; Mark 5:25-34

- The Syrophoenician Woman: Matthew 15:21-28; Mark 7:24-30
- The Samaritan Woman: John 4
- Priscilla: Acts 18:2-3; Romans 16:3-5; 1 Corinthians 16:19; 2 Timothy 4:19
- Phoebe: Romans 16:1-2
- Lydia: Acts 16:14-15
- Dorcas: Acts 9:36-42
- Joan: Luke 8:1-3; Luke 24:10
- Rhoda: Hechos 12:12-15
- The Woman with the Spirit of Sickness Luke 13:10-17
- The Adulterous Woman John 8:1-11
- Susan: Luke 8:3
- Eunice and Lois: 2 Timothy 1:5
- Junias: Romans 16:7

2. **Other Comments and Observations:**

- Eve: Her disobedience led to original sin, but she is also seen as the mother of all humanity.
- Sarah: Her faith was tested over many years of infertility before she gave birth to Isaac.
- Rebekah: Her decision to leave her home to marry Isaac shows her willingness to follow God's plan.
- Rachel and Leah: Their struggles and rivalries within the polygamous marriage with Jacob have lessons about family and reconciliation.
- Miriam: As Moses' sister, she played a key role in the story of Israel's deliverance.
- Deborah: She was an exceptional leader in an age dominated by men, showing courage and faith in God.
- Jael: His decisive action to kill Sisera freed Israel from Canaanite oppression.
- Ruth: Their story of loyalty and redemption is a powerful testimony to God's love and providence.
- Hannah: Your fervent prayer and the birth of Samuel show the importance of faith and devotion.

- Rahab: Her faith and courage in protecting Israelite spies place her in the genealogy of Jesus.
- Esther: Her courage and wisdom saved the Jewish people from destruction.
- The Widow of Zarephath: Her faith in times of scarcity is an example of trust in God's provision.
- The Shunammite Woman: Her hospitality and faith led to the resurrection of her son.
- Mary (mother of Jesus): Her obedience and humility made possible the birth of Jesus, the Savior.
- Martha: Her concern for service and faith in Jesus at the time of her brother Lazarus' death.
- Mary of Bethany: Her act of adoration and preparation for the tomb of Jesus is a testimony of her devotion.
- The Woman with Issue of Blood: Her faith in touching Jesus' garment and being healed is a powerful lesson in faith and perseverance.
- The Canaanite Woman: Her persistence in faith shows the importance of humility and trust in Jesus.
- The Samaritan Woman: Her encounter with Jesus reveals the extension of the gospel message to all peoples.
- Mary Magdalene: Her witness to the resurrection of Jesus makes her the first to proclaim the gospel.
- Priscilla: Your role in teaching and supporting Paul in ministry underscores the importance of collaboration in faith.
- Phoebe: As a deaconess, her service and leadership reflect the crucial role of women in the early church.
- Lydia: Her conversion and hospitality show how the gospel spread in Europe.
- Abigail: Your wisdom and diplomacy saved your family from David's wrath.
- Elizabeth: Her miraculous pregnancy and response of faith highlight the fulfillment of God's promises.
- The Widow with the Two Whites: Her extreme generosity in the midst of poverty illustrates the true spirit of giving.

## Important observation

The appendices provide additional resources to deepen the study and understanding of biblical women and their impact on redemptive history. References and documents help place each figure in context, highlighting valuable lessons and the relevance of their faith and actions to believers today.

# *GLOSSARY*

1. **Worship**: Expression of reverence, love, and devotion to God. It is a total response of the heart, mind, and body to God's majesty. (Reference: Psalm 95:6).
2. **Faith**: Trust and firm belief in God and His promises, without the need for physical testing. It is the certainty of what is expected and the conviction of what is not seen. (Reference: Hebrews 11:1).
3. **Obedience**: The act of following God's will and commandments. It is a sign of love and respect for God, and it is fundamental to the Christian life. (Reference: John 14:15).
4. **Redemption**: Deliverance from the power of sin and death through the sacrifice of Jesus Christ. It is the act by which God saves sinners and grants them eternal life. (Reference: Ephesians 1:7).
5. **Providence**: God's care and guidance over all His creatures. It is God's way of sustaining and directing all things in the universe. (Reference: Romans 8:28).
6. **Courage**: Courage and determination to face danger, adversity, or challenges, trusting in God's help and strength. (Reference: Joshua 1:9).
7. **Hospitality**: Practice of receiving and serving guests and visitors with generosity and kindness. It is a Christian virtue that demonstrates love and concern for others. (Reference: 1 Peter 4:9).
8. **Wisdom**: Ability to discern and correctly apply knowledge and experience to make fair and prudent decisions. It is considered a gift from God. (Reference: James 1:5).
9. **Peace**: A state of tranquility and harmony, both internal and external, that comes from a right relationship with God and with others. (Reference: Matthew 5:9).

10. **Service**: The act of working with and helping others, especially in a Christian context, where one serves God by serving others. (Reference: Galatians 5:13).
11. **Loyalty**: Fidelity and constancy in commitments and relationships. In the Bible, Ruth's loyalty to Naomi and God's faithfulness to His people are highlighted. (Reference: Ruth 1:16-17).
12. **Resurrection**: The fact of returning to life after death. In the Christian context, it refers especially to the resurrection of Jesus, which is the basis of the Christian hope of eternal life. (Reference: 1 Corinthians 15:20).
13. **Genealogy**: A record of the ancestors and descents of a person or family. In the Bible, genealogies are important to show the fulfillment of God's promises through the generations. (Reference: Matthew 1:1-17).
14. **Legacy**: Lasting impact and the lessons a person leaves for future generations. In the biblical context, it refers to the spiritual and moral heritage passed down through faith and actions. (Reference: 2 Timothy 1:5).

# BIBLIOGRAPHY

Brenner. Athalya. 1994. *The role of women in the Bible*. Editorial Ray. 1994.

Brown. Cheryl. 2008. *Women in the Old Testament*. Kairós Publishing. 2008.

Craig. A. Evans. 2002. *The Cultural Background of the Bible*. Editorial Vida. 2002.

Erickson, Millard J. 2014. *Systematic Theology*. Publisher: Editorial Vida. 2014.

Fee. Gordon D. 2001. *The exegesis of the New Testament*. Editorial Clie. 2001.

Glahn. Sandra. 2010. *The influence of women in the New Testament*. Editorial Zondervan. 2010.

Grudem. Wayne. 2007. *Systematic Theology:* An Introduction to Biblical Doctrine Editorial Vida. 2007.

Heim. Knut Martin. 2013. Poetry and Prophecy in the Old Testament. Westminster Publisher, John Knox Press. 2013.

Jeremiah. Joachim. 1998. *Jerusalem in the Time of Jesus*. Editorial FCE, 1998.

Keller. Timothy. 2013. *Preaching: How to Preach with Power Clarity*. Editorial Vida. 2013.

Lima Socarrás, José Arnaldo. *Celebrating Every Day with Jesus*. [Editorial Renacer].

Meyers. Carol. 2000. *Women in the Hebrew Bible*. Oxford University Press. 2000.

Mollenkott. Virginia R.1987. *Women, men and God.* Eerdmans Publishing. 1987.

Piper. John. *The Joy of Obeying God: Chosen by His Grace*. Unilit Publishing. 2015.

Reina-Valera. 1960 version. *Sacred Bible*.

Richards. Lawrence O. 2006. *Bible dictionary for young people.* Editorial Caribe. 2006.

Stott, John R. W. 2014. *The Cross of Christ.* Editorial Spokesman. 2014.

Sproul. R. C. 2017. *The Holiness of God.* Editorial Unilit, 2017.

Strong. James. 2002. *Strong's Dictionary of Original Words from the Old and New Testaments.* Editorial Caribe. 2002.

Tamez. Elsa. 1996. *Women in the Jesus Movement.* Editorial CLAI. 1996.

Trimm. Charlie. 2016. *The role of women in the formation of Israel.* Editorial Baker Academic, 2016.

Tozer. A. W. 2016. *The Search for God.* Editorial CLIE, 2016.

Wright. N. T. 2003. *The resurrection of the Son of God.* Editorial Fortress Press. 2003.

Witherington III. Ben. 1987. *Women in the Ministry of Jesus.* Abingdon Press, 1987.

# AUTHOR BIOGRAPHY

**José Arnaldo Lima Socarrás**, is pastor and founder of the Evangelical Ministry of Jesus Christ: "Reborn for a living hope". Since the age of 18, he has dedicated his life to preaching the gospel, accumulating more than 25 years of ministry. His preaching has resonated not only in Cuba, his homeland, but also in several Latin American countries, including Ecuador, Colombia, Panama, Costa Rica, Nicaragua, Honduras, Guatemala, Mexico, and the United States.

### Education and Career

*José Lima Socarrás*, trained as an Agronomist Technician before answering the call to pastoral ministry, completing his theological studies at the Theological Seminary in Matanzas, Cuba. His passion for the gospel and commitment to God's call have led him to establish churches, preach at conferences and seminars, and provide comfort and exhortation to countless people.

### Works and Contributions

In addition to his pastoral ministry, José is a prolific composer and author. He has produced several albums of Christian music that have touched hearts and glorified God. Among his books are titles that address issues essential to Christian life, theology, and spirituality. His works have inspired and strengthened the faith of many believers.

Some of his most notable works include:

- ❖ *Friends of God*

- *Growing in Grace*
- *The Beatitudes: A Necessity Today*
- *Faith: A Reason for Life*
- *Celebrating Every Day with Jesus*
- *Proverbs: Today as Yesterday*

**International Ministry**

José Socarrás' ministry has crossed borders, bringing the gospel message to diverse cultures and contexts. His focus on church planting and discipleship has left a lasting impact on the communities where he has served. Through his preaching, teaching, and writing, he has reached many lives, bringing them to the feet of Jesus and helping them grow in their faith.

**Personal Life**

José is married to Luz María Barrera, his wife and friend. Together, they reside in Florida, United States, where they continue their ministry and enjoy their family life. Joseph's dedication to his family is as strong as his commitment to his pastoral calling, and both aspects of his life reflect his love and devotion to God.

José Arnaldo Lima Socarrás is a man dedicated to God, whose life and work are testimony to his faith and passion for the gospel. Their mission is to inspire and guide others in their Christian walk, providing tools and teachings that strengthen their relationship with God.

# WORKS OF THE AUTHOR

**José Arnaldo Lima Socarrás,** is a pastor and author committed to teaching and edifying the church through his writings. His focus on practical theology and his dedication to daily Christian life have impacted many people, leading them toward a deeper faith and a more intimate relationship with God.

Pastor Lima Socarrás has written a series of books that address a variety of topics crucial to the Christian life, theology, and spirituality. His work has been a source of inspiration and guidance for many believers.

Below is a list of his publications:

1. **"Friends of God"**
    - An in-depth look at biblical friendships and their relevance to Christians today.
2. **"Growing in Grace"**
    - It explores how believers can grow in God's grace and knowledge.
3. **"The Beatitudes: A Necessity Today"**
    - A detailed study of the beatitudes and their practical application in modern life.
4. **"Faith: A Reason for Life"**
    - Reflections and teachings on the importance of faith in the Christian life.
5. **"Celebrating Every Day with Jesus"**
    - Daily devotionals that inspire you to live a Christ-centered life.
6. **"Proverbs: Today as Yesterday"**
    - An analysis of biblical proverbs and their timeless wisdom.
7. **"The Day to Day in the Life of the Christian"**
    - Practical guide to living the Christian faith daily.
8. **"The 7 Churches of the Apocalypse"**

- An in-depth study of the letters to the seven churches in the book of Revelation.

9. **"12 Hindrances to Effective Prayer"**
    - Identification and overcoming of obstacles in the believer's prayer life.
10. **"A Life-Changing Doctrine**
    - Fundamental teachings of Christian doctrine that transform life.
11. **"The Doctrine That Can Be Believed"**
    - He defends the soundness of Christian doctrine in a skeptical world.
12. **"Jesus Christ: Source of Grace and Life"**
    - It explores the centrality of Christ in Christian life and faith.
13. **"The Church belongs to Jesus Christ"**
    - A study of the nature and purpose of the church.
14. **"How to be safe"**
    - Teachings on assurance of salvation and trust in God.
15. **"Grace as a Reward for Grace"**
    - Reflections on the nature of God's grace and its impact on our lives.
16. **"Song of Songs"**
    - A poetic and spiritual analysis of the book of Song of Songs.
17. **"Love One Another"**
    - The importance of brotherly love in the Christian community.
18. **"Getting to Know the Bible Better"**
    - Tools and methods for deeper Bible study.
19. **"The Israel of Promise"**
    - Study on Israel's Role in Redemptive History.
20. **"The Spirit of the Lord Is Upon Me"**
    - Reflections on the ministry and anointing of the Holy Spirit.
21. **"The Great I Am"**
    - Exploration of God's names and attributes.

22. **"I want to be like Jesus"**
    - A children's book that includes stories, Bible verses, and activities to learn about the life of Jesus.
23. **"I follow Jesus: His footsteps"**
    - Stories and teachings about following Jesus and living according to his teachings.
24. **"Coloring Christmas"**
    - A children's book with Christmas stories, Bible verses, prayers, and coloring activities.
25. **"Walking with Noah and the Animals on the Ark"**
    - Children's story about Noah and the Ark, with interactive activities.
26. **"My Honda is David's"**
    - Story and reflection on David's courage and faith, adapted for children.
27. **"The Mother of the Word"**
    - An in-depth theological study of Mary, the mother of Jesus, from a Reformed perspective.
28. **"Small Hearts, Great in Faith"**
    - Series of children's devotionals to cover the whole year.
29. **"Know Him by His Names"**
    - Explore the names and attributes of God, Jesus, and the Holy Spirit.
30. **"God of Covenants"**
    - Study on the biblical covenants and their theological significance.
31. **"The Path That Leads to Glory"**
    - Reflections and teachings on the Christian walk towards eternal glory.

# FINAL ENDPAPERS

## Invitation to Reading

You have walked a profound and transformative journey through the pages of "Women of the Bible: Strength, Faith, and Legacy." I hope this book has enriched your understanding of God and strengthened your faith. Each chapter has been an invitation to explore more deeply who God is, how He has revealed Himself in Scripture, and how we can consciously live under the reality of His promises in our daily lives.

## Final Thoughts

The knowledge that God is faithful and keeps his promises is not just a theological concept, but a lived truth that has the power to change our perspective and the way we live. It reminds us that God is always present, sufficient, and sovereign, and that we can trust Him at all times. As I close this book, I encourage you to continue to seek God, to deepen your relationship with Him, and to live each day with the assurance of His presence and power.

## Gratitude

I want to thank you for taking the time to read this book and allowing its truths to touch your heart. My prayer is that you have found in these pages inspiration, hope, and a renewed desire to follow God with your whole being.

## Testimony and Sharing

If this book has been a blessing to you, I invite you to share your testimony. How it has impacted your life, and how you have seen God work as the Great I Am. Your experiences can be a source of encouragement and edification for others. I also encourage you to share this book with friends, family, and members of your faith community, so that they too can know and experience God's transforming presence.

## *FINAL BLESSING*

*May the God of Abraham, Isaac, and Jacob bless you and keep you. May his face shine upon you and grant you peace. May His presence be your guide and strength in every moment of your life, and may you always live under the reality of His love and power.*

Amen.

*"DARE TO DREAM, TO BELIEVE, AND TO LIVE UNDER THE BLESSINGS OF ABRAHAM, ALLOW GOD'S FAITHFULNESS TO TRANSFORM EVERY AREA OF YOUR LIFE, AND DISCOVER A PATH FILLED WITH HOPE AND ETERNAL LOVE."*

## Embark on a Transformative Journey of Faith and Strength

"Women of the Bible: Strength, Faith, and Legacy" is not just a book; it is an invitation to experience the depth of God's life-changing promises from ancient times to today. José Arnaldo Lima Socarrás, pastor and dedicated author, takes you by the hand through a fascinating journey through Scripture, revealing how the promises made to Abraham continue to be a source of hope and transformation for believers today.

## Featured Chapters:

- ❖ Chapter 1: Eve - The Mother of All
- ❖ Chapter 2: Sarah - The Mother of Nations
- ❖ Chapter 3: Rebecca - A Woman of Decision
- ❖ Chapter 4: Rachel and Leah - Brotherhood and Rivalry
- ❖ Chapter 5: Miriam - Leadership and Worship
- ❖ Chapter 6: Deborah - The Prophetess and Judge
- ❖ Chapter 7: Ruth - Loyalty and Redemption
- ❖ Chapter 8: Hannah - Prayer and Promise
- ❖ Chapter 9: Esther - Courage and Providence
- ❖ Chapter 10: Mary - The Mother of Jesus

## Why is this book indispensable for your spiritual life?

- ❖ ***Discover Eternal Promises:***

    Step into the covenant God made with Abraham, a covenant that transcends generations and includes you. Experience the thrill of knowing that you are part of an eternal divine plan.

❖ **Live in Trust and Security:**

Learn how God's promises provide a solid foundation on which to build your life, offering peace and certainty even in times of uncertainty.

❖ **Inspiration and Real Testimonials:**

Read contemporary stories of people whose lives have been transformed by trusting in God's promises. Let their testimonies motivate you to live with renewed faith.

❖ **Practical Applications and Study Guide:**

Equipped with practical tools and activities, this book not only teaches you about God's promises, but also shows you how to apply them in your daily life to live with purpose and hope.

❖ **A Call to Action**:

Don't pass up the opportunity to discover how God's promises to Abraham can transform your life. This book challenges you to live each day with the assurance that God is faithful and that His promises are true. Through deep insights and simple practices, "**Women of the Bible: Strength, Faith, and Legacy**" will help you strengthen your faith and find a new sense of purpose and direction.

Made in United States
Cleveland, OH
14 February 2025